COME
AND
SEE

WHAT PEOPLE ARE SAYING

"There are stories and then there are *stories*. Proem has one of those – a riveting, unbelievable, life-changing, nation-altering, only-God story. Read this book, soak in the story, and be inspired to join Proem in their mission of loving people, meeting needs, and pointing everyone to Jesus."

—**Kyle Idleman**, Senior Pastor, Southeast Christian Church

"I have known, admired and partnered with Maui Dwulat and the Proem Ministry in Poland for decades and my only regret is that we didn't meet sooner! Proem is a front-line Kingdom force that is making a difference through the intentional pursuit of the Great Commission of Jesus with the compassion that Jesus said would distinguish everyone who follows Him. Consequently, the impact of Proem is life-changing throughout Eastern Europe and beyond! Teams from Compassion Christian Church serve in Poland with Proem every Summer. We have partnered with their ministry to students, war refugees, athletes and Christmas and Easter Outreach, efforts that have reached hundreds of thousands of Polish people with the Gospel of Jesus. Proem has hosted our Refresh Retreats where we bring our Global Mission Partners and their families to Poland from around the world for a time of rest, encouragement and restoration! I hope this book enables you to not only see what God is doing through Proem...but inspires you to come and be a part of it!"

—**Cam Huxford**, Lead Pastor, Compassion Christian Church

"For the last several decades I have been inspired by the work of Proem Ministries in Poland. When I have been onsite with them at camp, a church facility or school, everything they do is intentional and powerfully points people to Jesus. And when I am an ocean away their social media posts keep me connected, praying and believing for God's great work around the world. I hope everyone reads this book!

—**Todd Clark**, Teaching Pastor, Parkview Christian Church

"Maui is one in a million. A special guy with a big heart and a brilliant mind. What he and his team has accomplished in Poland is a miracle. I have been blessed to see it firsthand as I have traveled to Poland five times. Enjoy reading this amazing book!

—**Douglas J Crozier**, CEO of The Solomon Foundation

"I have been associated with Maui Dwulat and Proem Ministries for over twenty years though the ministry of Mount Pleasant Christian Church. Proem is much more than just a ministry partner, it's a place where lives are being changed by the love of Jesus. From the many different camps for students and families, to the schools, to the community outreach, to the commitment to planting churches Proem is involved in changing the world for Christ. I thank God for Maui's leadership that flows from his deep commitment to Christ."

—**Chris Philbeck**, Senior Pastor,
Mount Pleasant Christian Church

"I have known of and supported Proem from a long distance for a long time. Then I went to Poland – twice – and was able to see what they do up close, I became a raving fan. Their ministry is incredible and when you read this book, you'll discover the story leading up to it is equally amazing!"

—**Vince Antonucci**, Pastor and Author of
God For The Rest Of Us

The Story Of PROEM

COME

AND

SEE

An Adventure with God

Told by MAUI DWULAT

Written by VINCE ANTONUCCI

FOREWORD BY BOB RUSSELL

INDIE BOOKS
INTERNATIONAL

COME AND SEE
An Adventure with God

ISBN-13: 978-1-957651-82-8

Library of Congress Control Number: 2024914875

Designed by Melissa Farr, Back Porch Creative, LLC

INDIE BOOKS INTERNATIONAL®, INC.
2511 WOODLANDS WAY
OCEANSIDE, CA 92054
www.indiebooksintl.com

TABLE OF CONTENTS

FOREWORD

by Bob Russell
May 2024

Have you ever noticed how many *it just so happened* incidents there are in the Bible? Isaac's servant was searching for a wife for his master and sat down to take a break at a watering hole. *It just so happened* that the lovely Rebekah came to water her father's camels, and within days, Isaac and Rebekah were married.

Joseph's brothers beat him up and threw him into a cistern, intending to let him die of exposure. But *it just so happened* that a band of Ishmaelite traders came by at that very moment. The brothers decided to sell Joseph to them as a slave, and the teenage boy, who was his father's favorite, was carted off to Egypt. A most dramatic chapter of Jewish history was about to unfold!

Ruth was gleaning in a grain field, trying to garner enough to eat for herself and her mother-in-law. But *it just so happened* that Boaz, the field's owner, a wealthy bachelor, took notice of her, and an exciting, life-changing romance began.

The virgin Mary was told she was to give birth to the Messiah. But Mary was from Nazareth, and the Messiah was prophesied to be born in Bethlehem. And *it just so happened* that a decree went out from Caesar Augustus that all the world was to be taxed. So Joseph took Mary, his fiancé, and headed for Bethlehem, his original hometown, to register. "And while they were there, the time came for the baby to be born" (Luke 2:6).

Paul and Silas were imprisoned in Philippi for disturbing the peace. But at midnight, *it just so happened* that an earthquake shook open the prison gates and freed them from their shackles. When the missionaries didn't flee, the jailer and his family became believers and were baptized in the middle of the night.

Popular preacher and author J. Wallace Hamilton once wrote about a mother cat with a tiny kitten in her mouth, trying to get across a busy New York City intersection. She'd dart into the street, nearly hit by a honking car, and dash back to the sidewalk. A softhearted traffic cop saw her plight and put up his hands to halt traffic in both directions. The mother cat then scurried across the street and disappeared down an alleyway.

Hamilton pointed out the cat had no idea that the power of the New York City Police Department was the reason she got up to get her safely across. Then he added, "I wonder how many times the powerful hand of the Almighty goes up to protect us or get us safely to the appropriate destination, and we're not even aware of it." What we assume is a mere coincidence is a God-incident in which he directs our path.

Full disclosure—I'm not a hyper-Calvinist who believes that God predestines everything that happens. We are not puppets on a string. But I can look back at my life and see times when God intervened to direct my path when I wasn't even aware of it. I suspect you can, as well.

There's an old saying, "Big doors swing on small hinges." So many times, God uses small events and seemingly insignificant people to turn the tide of history. While the name Maui means "little" in Poland, God has used Maui Dwulat, the author of this book, in a huge way to impact his home country and others worldwide in recent years.

In the mid-nineties, I had what seemed an insignificant encounter with Maui. *It just so happened* he stopped by our church one Friday afternoon. And *it just so happened* he met Claudette Patton, our Missions Director. *It just so happened* that I was on campus, and Claudette introduced the two of us. Maui is one of those guys who is instantly likable and believable. He was humble, personable, and respectful. Well, *it just so happened* that I had nothing special planned for our Saturday morning Men's Bible study the next day, and I invited Maui to stop by for a brief, impromptu interview . . . something I rarely do.

It just so happened that Stan Franczek was attending Bible study that Saturday morning. God laid on Stan's heart to approach Maui afterward and ask him additional questions about his ministry. Stan is an unpretentious networker with numerous connections and access to resources. Stan shared Maui's vision for evangelizing Poland with others, and the Lord opened many doors through Stan's burgeoning relationship with Maui.

So when Maui Dwulat writes a book, *Come and See*, a story about how God used a little-known man with very few connections to do significant things in Poland, I promise you it's worth reading. Maui has a huge heart and a winsome personality. His passion for evangelism and extraordinary vision have been used by God to open huge doors for ministry. Proem, the mission he established 60 miles from Warsaw, has introduced thousands of Europeans to the Gospel. More recently, Proem ministered to thousands of desperate refugees fleeing from the war in Ukraine.

This book is more than an interesting autobiography; it's the thrilling story of how God works in surprising, seemingly insignificant ways to accomplish His will. Jesus spoke of a tiny mustard seed growing into a tree large enough for birds to build their nests. And Isaiah 55:8-9 assures us:

> "For my thoughts are not your thoughts,
>   neither are your ways my ways,"
>   declares the Lord.
> "As the heavens are higher than the earth,
>   so are my ways higher than your ways
>   and my thoughts than your thoughts.

Maui says when he looks at the history of Proem's ministry, he sees "a trail of miracles." He says he used to pray for open doors, but he doesn't pray that way anymore because the doors are wide open. Maui's vision has always been to see a need and meet that need. It might be through establishing youth camps, music teams, church plants, childcare, addiction counseling, grade schools, or refugee shelters. Proem continues to change methods without changing the message. The result has been one *it just so happened* event after another.

When we "*Come and See*" how God worked in the life of Maui Dwulat, it's encouraging because we can't help but conclude that if we're available and walk in His will, God can use us, too. Maybe you think it's a mere coincidence that you hold this book in your hand. But read it with a spirit of anticipation. *It may just so happen* that God may be working in the shadows to expand your vision and transform your future. "Big doors swing on small hinges!"

INTRODUCTION

The story of Proem is of small faith and a big God.

I want to share with you the story of what God has done through Proem in Poland. I must admit up front that I am a man of small faith. Fortunately, my small faith is in a big God, and Jesus said, "Truly I tell you, if you have faith as small as a mustard seed, you can say to this mountain, 'Move from here to there,' and it will move. Nothing will be impossible for you" (Matthew 17:20, NIV).

We learn from Jesus that what's essential is not having tremendous faith but putting our faith in a tremendous God. That's what I've done, and God has done more than I could have asked or imagined. What's happened is amazing, and it's all because of God. Yet it's also happened through:

- A group of incredible people who know Jesus and are willing to do whatever it takes to help everyone know Jesus.

- Supportive partners who are so committed to the mission of Jesus that they will sacrifice to see it happen, even in the small, faraway country of Poland.

Our Why And How

At Proem, we keep things intentionally simple. We exist to do three things: evangelize the lost, equip believers, and affect communities. Through years of experience (which you are going to read about), we have discovered that happens best when we do the following:

- Focus on people and their needs. We see a need and meet a need.

- Allow the methods to change, but always keep our message the same.

- Listen for God's whisper and look for what he's blessing, then go where God is leading and already working.

We are especially effective in our mission when we live by our three core values: relationships first, process over product, and team leadership.

By the end of this book, you'll see not only why all that is vital to us and how God has blessed it in often miraculous ways but also how you can live it out and see God work in your life.

Proem

Interestingly, in Polish, the word "prom"—Proem without the e—means "the ferry." A ferry is a ship that takes people from one side of a river to the other. We embrace the double meaning of

Proem/prom because, spiritually speaking, everything we do is to get people to the other side:

- From not knowing God's love to being filled with it
- From being far from Jesus to abiding in him
- From death to life
- From this life to heaven

What could be better, or more important, than that?

In the pages to come, you'll read the stories of how Proem started, the series of miracles that led to us owning a camp and a hotel, how we began starting churches and doing missions by mistake, God using sports and music in startling ways we never saw coming, starting a school and counseling ministry in response to needs in the community, God perfectly positioning us to care for a thousand refugees forced out of Ukraine by the Russian invasion, and the eternal difference God has allowed us to make in the lives of thousands and thousands of people.

What you are about to read may seem unbelievable, but it's all true. It's a story only God could author, a story he could write in your life if you put just some small faith in him.

chapter one

A Dream

I was eighteen years old.

I knew about dreams God gave people in the Bible.

He gave Abraham a vision that he would become a father of a great nation that would be a blessing to the world.

He gave Joseph a dream that he would be in a position of power and his brothers would bow down to him.

Jacob dreamed of a ladder stretching from earth to heaven, with angels descending and ascending and God promising to be with him and his offspring as they spread throughout the earth.

I want to be honest. I didn't have enough faith to dream a big dream, but I wanted it—the faith, the dream, the promise from God—all of it.

So, I prayed a simple, small prayer, "Lord, here's my life. Do you think you can do something with it? I'm available."

I never imagined what God would do with that prayer. I never imagined that someday I would be connected to Billy Graham, the Pope, or George Bush. I never imagined that someday the pastor of one of the biggest churches in America would put me in front of his people and ask me to share my vision. I never imagined that God would use me to start a ministry that would touch thousands of lives.

I never imagined. I had no idea of any of it.

And I don't take credit for any of the incredible things that have happened. It's all been God. God loves to use the foolish things of the world, and he is so great that small faith can lead to big things.

We just need to surrender ourselves to his will and be available. I hope this book inspires you to do exactly that.

But I'm getting ahead of myself.

The Beginnings Of Faith

I was privileged to grow up in a Christian home. I'm proud to be a third-generation Christian. Our son, Przemek, and his wife and their children are fourth- and fifth-generation evangelicals.

That is *highly* unusual in Poland. While Christianity has a history in Poland dating back to 966 AD, most Poles today have no or only a nominal faith. It's estimated that only 25 percent are actively engaged in a church and nearly all of that is in the Catholic

Church. Our population is approximately 40 million and less than 0.2 percent are evangelical Christians.

How did I grow up with Christian parents?

Back in 1914, at about the time World War I broke out and when the nation of Poland did not officially exist, both sets of my grandparents went on a crusade. They walked in as young adults with a very nominal Catholic faith, heard an itinerant preacher, and left, having put their faith in Jesus as their savior.

So, my parents, who were born in the 1920s, grew up in a Christian home.

I am the fourth child in my family, which is how I got the nickname "Maui," a Polish word for "little one." Yes, I am the small one with small faith in a big God.

Church was a big part of my family life. If the church was open—Sunday mornings, Sunday evenings, Wednesday evenings— we were there.

When I was a child, my mother, who was only forty-one, had a fatal stroke in our backyard. My father carried her to our house. Her arm was hanging down, and I remember desperately trying to help by holding her hand. We got in the house and my father put her on the couch. In our shock, we didn't know what to do, so we prayed for a miracle. The next morning, I quietly opened the door and peeked through the crack to see if she was still on the couch, hoping that she might be well enough to have gotten up. But she was now in a dress, still lying there, but instead of on the couch, she was in a casket.

Our small church of about forty people rallied around us, but it was a very difficult time for our family.

I was ten years old and wrestled with questions. "Why is this happening? Why us? We go to church; we are good people, dedicated Christians." For years, I struggled to make sense of it. Though my faith was fragile, I never strayed too far off the path of what I had been taught at home and church. I still believed, but I wasn't experiencing a personal relationship with God.

Eventually, my father remarried, so I had a stepmother. Then, I moved about seventy miles from home to go to high school. I lived in the dorm. It was too big, and too noisy, and there was too much unknown for a fifteen-year-old having to live away from his family. I was the only evangelical in the school of approximately one thousand students. My faith was still only intellectual and shaky, and I was not courageous enough to share it with my new friends. They all went to Catholic churches on Sundays and would ask where I went, but it was difficult for me to be brave enough to explain why I went to a different church or why I had my own Bible.

All that changed when I went to camp in the middle of high school. My brother and I went to the small Christian camp every summer since I was thirteen. I was eighteen when something transformative happened within me at that camp. I truly made a decision for Jesus and surrendered the rest of my life to God. That's when I prayed the prayer I now believe ignited everything, "Lord, here's my life. Do you think you can do something with it? I'm available."

The Beginnings Of Ministry

Back at school, I started giving Bibles to some of my friends.

I learned you have to be careful who you give a Bible to because it can change not only their lives but yours.

How?

One of the friends I gave a Bible to was a beautiful girl named Ewa, whom I married a few years later.

Before we met, Ewa was not a believer. She was raised by a father who was high up in the Community Party and who had little use for Christianity. Ewa received the Bible, started reading it, and eventually made her decision for Christ. She told her parents, who were so upset that Ewa had to leave home.

After high school, I moved to Warsaw to attend seminary. Ewa followed me to Warsaw, where she attended the university to study education. We got married and started a family while we were still attending school.

I enrolled in seminary, certain that God was calling me to ministry but unsure what it might look like. Ewa and I became involved in campus ministry where it became obvious we would eventually work with young people in some way.

chapter two

WINDS OF CHANGE

L ooking back, it strikes me that early in my ministry, I did what I knew. My grandparents' lives were changed at an evangelistic event, and in the beginning, I put on evangelistic events. My life was changed at a camp, and in the beginning, I put on camps.

But as Poland slowly opened, so did my methods.

Jesus told a parable of a farmer who indiscriminately scattered seed. It seems he just threw seed everywhere. Some seeds fell on rocky soil, where they instantly died. Some fell into shallow soil, where they shot up, but the life was quickly snuffed out of them by the heat of the sun. Other seeds fell in good, deep soil, where they took root, grew, and produced a harvest.

I learned some important truths from Jesus's parable:

- In the parable, the seeds represent the Gospel, and the farmer is throwing a *lot* of seeds. We need to be sharing the Gospel as often as possible with as many people as possible.

- The seeds are not just planted in one small patch of ideal soil; they are thrown everywhere, even in seemingly unfavorable locations. We need to share the Gospel everywhere, even with people who may not seem very receptive.

- The soil matters. In the parable, the seed is all the same. What changes and is the determining factor is the receptivity of the soil. The same is true when we share Jesus with people.

- The harvest is not immediate. When you plant a pumpkin seed, you don't get an instant pumpkin. It takes time for the seed to take root and for the fruit to grow. Some Christians expect to see instant results from one spiritual conversation with a stranger, but if we play out Jesus's parable, we would expect a spiritual harvest to be the result of a process, and probably not a quick one.

I discovered the reality of all those truths firsthand as I continued in ministry and tried new methods of sharing the Gospel, much of which was possible because of what was happening in Poland.

A Change In The Government

You could almost smell the fresh wind of change in Poland. A breeze was blowing through the country and bringing hope.

In the early 1980s, the Communists began to see that their time in control was nearing an end, so they instituted martial law. Everything was rationed. Citizens had to use coupons for food, coffee, baby food, diapers, etc.

Churches around the world started sending everyday essentials to our church in Poland, and we were able to pass them on to our neighbors. These efforts by the church were well received. People were confused why we weren't keeping everything for ourselves and asked, "Why are you doing this?" which gave us the opportunity to share Jesus.

I was able to develop many relationships by distributing goods, especially with the health department and local drug stores. Many of those relationships are still active today. It was a great way to build trust and earn credibility in the community. We were preparing the soil and, whenever we could, planting seeds.

Eventually, as the Solidarity Movement gained momentum, Communism fell. On December 9, 1990, Lech Wałęsa was elected president. The change in leadership took place relatively quickly, but the new leadership lacked experience. The people thought that now that we have a democracy, we can do everything like the Western world. But Poland and its new leadership were not ready. In fact, people were upset that progress happened slowly and, in the next election, voted in a former Communist Party leader. They expected too much too quickly, not understanding that a harvest is rarely immediate.

A Change In Our Ministry

The change in government is part of what led to the founding of Proem.

People in Poland were coming out of Communism and open to new things. Yet most Poles were still *not* open to an evangelical church. If a church was not Catholic, it was viewed as a cult.

We knew the fields were ripe for harvest, and we needed to sow seeds. We decided we could do so more effectively if we were a not-for-profit organization rather than a church. In a way, we were trying to follow the example of the Apostle Paul, who said, "I have become all things to all people so that by all possible means I might save some. I do all this for the sake of the Gospel, that I may share in its blessings" (1 Corinthians 9:22–23).

At first, our ministry was affiliated with an international camps ministry called Word of Life Bible Institute, which still exists today. Our primary ministry was providing camps for young people. At each camp, I was upfront about being a pastor and invited the campers and their parents to our church.

In 1990, we opened our first office in downtown Warsaw. The camps were successful, but we knew we had to sow more seeds.

We started passing out tracts with the message of salvation. At that time, people were so excited about their newfound freedom that they would stop and take anything anyone was offering.

It was easy to draw a crowd. We began setting up sketch boards in front of our office and presenting Jesus with paintings and drawings. People were open and would listen.

At the time, there was freedom for everything, and people were open to anything. New philosophies, new nightclubs, people wanted new.

Much like Jesus's parable, we were able to cast lots of seed and saw it fall on both good and bad soil.

Our message was well received by many.

Just like in Jesus's parable, some seeds took root, grew, and produced a harvest. Some embraced the Gospel and started coming to church. Our church, of about eighty people during Communism, grew to well over 500 fairly quickly during democracy. We planted a new campus in another part of Warsaw.

But other seed fell on the soil in which it did not last. In their excitement for all things new, many were open to the Gospel but soon became distracted by other things.

Others rejected us altogether.

Regardless, we just kept sowing seed and trying to water it.

We continued to host camps, but because we didn't have adequate facilities, many who wanted to come couldn't because there wasn't room.

Our team wanted to create spaces outside the church for people to connect and have spiritual conversations, so we rented spaces in restaurants, tea houses, and coffee shops.

We learned from all these new experiences, and they helped form our strategies for sharing the Gospel in the future.

We also realized at this time that we had lots of *learning* and work to do and that we *needed a camp of our own* because we had lots of kids who wanted to come.

Ewa was working as a teacher; she graduated from the university at the same time as I graduated from the seminary. As students, we were involved in campus ministry. It became obvious that we would spend time working with young people.

After seminary, I was worked as a youth pastor for a church. We were doing camps for young people on our church property, including basketball camps.

The Beginnings Of The End Of Communism In Poland

For the first nine years after we graduated, Poland remained a Communist country. Faith in God was frowned upon, and evangelism was virtually forbidden.

But there was a light at the end of the tunnel.

Uprisings occurred occasionally in Poland, but none ever succeeded. But the Solidarity Movement, founded by Lech Wałęsa, was better organized than any before it.

The government slowly loosened its reins on what churches were permitted to do. We decided to take advantage of this newfound freedom and ask the government for permission to host a summer rally for young people.

Four days before the event was to begin, we still didn't have approval to have it, and I was called into the police station. I didn't know what to expect. I sat in the waiting room along with about fifteen other people. Finally, my name was called, and I walked into a small, plain room with just a desk and two chairs. I was so nervous.

The police captain growled, "Tell me more about this conference." I tried to smile and told him I didn't know he wanted to talk about our event, or I would have brought our materials. The captain reached into his drawer and pulled out all the materials we had prepared.

The captain continued with questions about the various speakers, asking what each would be speaking about.

The first time, I answered, "He will be talking about God and the Bible and how Jesus came to save the world. How Jesus died for you and me."

The captain moved on to the next speaker, "What will he be talking about?"

I said, "He will also be talking about God and the Bible and how Jesus came to save the world, how he died for you and me."

He asked about the next speaker, and I repeated the same answer.

Eventually, I convinced the captain everything would be peaceful, and he gave us permission to host the rally. I even invited him to attend the conference. He replied, "You don't have to invite me. I will be there, and my people will be there as well. And if something goes wrong, we *will* intervene."

We had between four and five thousand young people attend our rally. Authorities mingled among the crowd, and troops were at the ready, but everything was peaceful. The captain was there for every session and, at the end of the event, told me, "I admire you. You had four thousand young people in one place, and they didn't create any trouble. It is unbelievable how you can control the crowd without making a riot."

I thought back to the way it had been in the 1960s when it was dangerous to be a Christian, and we were not allowed to do evangelism. Our mindset had been that we were lucky the government allowed us to meet in our churches and have Bibles to read. But now we were openly sharing Jesus, and Communist officials were there watching it happen.

Winds of change were blowing—in our country and in my life.

chapter three

WHAT TO DO WHILE YOU ARE WAITING

No one likes to wait. I certainly don't. I like things to happen when I want them to happen. *Now* is my favorite time.

The problem is that God likes for us to wait. Why? We almost never know, but he does.

The word "wait" appears in the Bible about 150 times.

Abraham, Joseph, and Jacob had to wait years for the dreams God gave them to be fulfilled.

Jesus had to wait thirty years before launching his ministry.

We're encouraged to "Wait for the Lord; be strong and take heart and wait for the Lord" (Psalm 27:14). It's a beautiful verse, but no one likes waiting.

Yet waiting is exactly what we found ourselves doing. We had launched our ministry, and things were going well, especially in our camps. The issue was that we had limited space. We needed to purchase a campground of our own so we could have more kids and sow more seeds.

We started looking but—nothing.

We kept looking and—nothing.

I asked God to respond as I prayed the prayer of Jabez, "Oh, that you would bless me and enlarge my territory!" (1 Chronicles 4:10).

We kept looking—nothing.

Occasionally, something would come up—a property that seemed right for us. Our excitement would rise and we felt convinced this was God's answer, but every time some obstacle would pop up at the last moment preventing us from finalizing a deal.

We looked for ten years. Ten years is a long time to wait. But God promises, "Wait for the Lord and keep his way. He will exalt you to inherit the land" (Psalm 37:34 ESV).

Perhaps you're waiting—waiting for God to provide something you feel you're lacking, for God to give you an opportunity you've been wanting, for God to expand your ministry's impact.

Sometimes, God knows it's best for us to wait.

So, what do we do while we're waiting?

We *trust God,* and we learn.

We Learn

Waiting is an amazing opportunity to grow. As I look back at our years of wandering in the wilderness, waiting for God to show us our "promised land," I am so grateful for the chance it gave us to learn.

We learned as we did camps on church property and experimented with new ministries and ways of sharing the Gospel.

However, the education that shaped how we eventually did ministry began years earlier.

In 1962, a Polish evangelist named George Bajenski went to America to study, where he met with some respected Christian leaders. He came back to Poland in 1984, where I was getting started as a youth minister in the church in Warsaw. George brought some American preachers. One was Jack Wyrtzen, founder of Word of Life Bible Institute ministries. He asked if I would like to travel to America to study for a year. I was skeptical, wondering if he was just being nice. Three months later, I received a formal invitation. Everything would be paid for except our travel to and from the United States.

I was excited to go but felt uncertain whether it could really happen. At that time, Polish people's passports were kept by the police and only given if the Communist government approved travel out of the country.

At the end of 1985, we received our passports and student visas. We sold our car and bought open-ended round-trip tickets. On January 6, 1986, we flew from Warsaw to Montreal, Canada.

In Montreal, Bajenski picked us up and drove four hours south of Montreal to the small town of Pottersville in upstate New York. It was our first time in America. When we landed and drove through the Adirondack Mountains, walls of snow stared ominously down at us at every turn, making us wonder if we had really been taken to Siberia.

Three days after our arrival, I was sitting with five hundred other students in a vast auditorium, listening to a guest speaker from Canada. He was speaking machine gun rapid-fire fast. I leaned over and asked the person next to me, "What language is he speaking?" He looked at me for a second, then said, "English, of course."

I was overwhelmed.

My English was poor, and I felt pressure to learn a new language and a new culture. It wasn't easy, but eventually, we picked it up and felt more comfortable.

That year at the Word of Life Bible Institute in America was a powerful and practical learning experience. In my prior Bible college training in Poland, I had taken five years of Greek, four of Hebrew, and three of Latin. I took courses in the history of theology. What was missing was Bible training and help in practical ministry.

The Word of Life Bible Institute in America was predominantly Bible training. We studied books of the Bible, memorized Scriptures, had guest speakers teach the Bible, and took three tests a week. I loved all of it.

God provided all kinds of new relationships. We had no idea that some of those relationships would affect our ministry for decades to come.

I learned many important lessons that year that eventually helped shape our ministry in Poland.

Be Practical

In Poland, I learned theology, which is important. But in America, I was taught to apply the Scripture to everyday life. For example, Jesus spoke of his followers ministering to prisoners, but in Poland, I never actually lived this out by visiting a prison. I went twice in my year in America. I was able to share my testimony—because I had learned that no one can argue with your story—and then tell the prisoners about Jesus.

In our preaching class, we were taught effective speaking styles and how to make real-life applications in our sermons. Then, we had to write and preach sermons to the other students in our class. The sermons were recorded so we could watch and talk about them later.

The Power Of Relationships

I was also taught to value relationships in ministry. I not only listened to my teachers and guest speakers but also met and talked with them outside of class.

I spent time with Charles Ryrie, a famous Bible translator, and W. A. Criswell, the well-known author and pastor of the First Baptist Church in Dallas. Building relationships with respected Christian leaders was huge for a young youth pastor from Warsaw,

Poland. Jack Wyrtzen, the founder of the Word of Life Bible Institute, invited married students and their spouses to his house every Thursday for supper and to have some time to talk to him. You never forget that.

Adapting

My wife and I, along with our four-year-old son Przemek, had to adjust to life in a completely different culture. One day, my son declared America "a weird country." I asked why, and he explained, "In the winter, you walk into the house to get warm. In the summer, you walk into the house to get cold." We had never experienced air conditioning or much of anything "American" before.

The process of having to learn a culture and adapt to it taught us valuable lessons we would apply to ministry in a rapidly changing culture in Poland in the years that followed.

Fun And Relevance

Camps in Poland were small—typically fifty kids or maybe one hundred at the biggest camps. The goal of those camps was to cram as much Bible teaching in as possible.

In America, the size and approach were different. Camps were fun, and relevant to the campers' lives. The camp operators still shared Jesus and taught the Bible, but they knew they could get more kids to come—especially those who were far from God—by making camp fun.

One year and one day after leaving Warsaw, we returned. A customs worker checked our passports and asked, "Are you returning to Poland?" We said, "Yes." He asked, "Didn't you like America?" We told him, "We love America, but we are coming back!"

He smiled, stamped our passports, and welcomed us home.

We didn't know what was in store, but we knew we were returning to let the Lord lead us on the next path he had for us.

We Work

What do you do while you're waiting? You trust God, you learn, and you *work*.

When we returned to Poland, I assumed my opportunities to use what I learned about ministry would be limited because the old system still controlled it. But two years later, democracy took over, and with it, new opportunities.

The Billy Graham Evangelistic Association

With Poland's new openness, I started working with the Billy Graham Evangelistic Association. They set up a satellite mission where crusades were delivered in different languages. Our downtown Warsaw office became the information center for seventy-plus crusade sites in Poland.

I traveled around the country meeting with local organizers and later became chairman of the association's committee in Poland. That was a huge opportunity to connect with pastors, bishops, and even people from the Catholic Church. When Billy Graham died in 2018, I was one of two Polish people invited to go to America for his funeral.

All of that gave me credibility as we built Proem. Working with all those churches and organizations outside our normal circle would also benefit Proem as we grew and gained support from other parts of the world.

Relational Ministry

I brought back from America an appreciation for relationships and the value of relational ministry. We knew we would meet people where they were, build connections, and meet their real needs.

One early example was chiropractors. In the early 1990s, chiropractic medicine was unknown in Poland. We had contacts with Christian chiropractors in America and invited them to Poland to use their skills for Jesus. They came and did "adjustments," which gave us the opportunity to build relationships and share the Gospel with people as they were waiting for their appointments.

We also began to use sports as another relational ministry. We tried to bring "outsiders" in with sports.

We organized basketball tournaments with thirty to forty teams signing up. During the competition, we would share the Gospel during a break.

Trying to fully become a part of the city we wanted to affect, we signed up a team for a citywide basketball league in Warsaw. There were more than two hundred teams, and we were the only Christian one. Our team was called "Pulaski Brothers" because our church was on Pulaski Street. We built great relationships with the other teams and, in 2000, we won first place. My nephew Daniel Wawrzyniak was the captain of the team. I served as the coach and chaplain, but after we won the city championship, I stepped down. You might as well leave on top.

Camps

Back in Poland, we continued to do camps, but we modified them in strategic ways.

We went from focusing on the quantity to the quality of Christian teaching.

We provided exciting sports, good food, and great music. If you are from America or have been to one of our camps in the last thirty years, that may sound normal, but at the time, it was revolutionary.

Ironically, we got pushback not from the government but from the church. Some in the older generation believed the students needed five hours of lectures a day and morning devotions at seven-thirty before breakfast. I reminded the church leadership that fourteen-to-sixteen-year-olds wake up hungry, and that we could start with breakfast and still make sure they got time for devotions and teaching. It took a while, but eventually, we got buy-in for our new approach.

Proem's ministry today has so many facets that it's hard for some to believe we began with a singular focus on camps. However, I believed we needed a successful anchor ministry to build from, and camps made sense. It was the one thing we had been doing for years because, even before the fall of Communism, camps were a great way to reach young people. I think of when God called Moses to ministry at the burning bush and asked him, "What is that in your hand?" (Exodus 4:2). Moses had been working as a shepherd for years. He replied, "A staff," and God used the staff. He used what Moses already had. We already had a camp ministry. We had experience in it and the community's trust. It was the perfect launching pad for Proem.

There was a problem. We had way more campers than camp! Registration would open, sign-ups would immediately flood in, and many would be disappointed that there was no space for them. Most of those disappointed young people did not know or have a relationship with Jesus and we were missing the opportunity to share him with them.

We decided we needed a permanent home for our camps. We were excited at the idea that God might provide one so we would have more space and wouldn't have to try and secure a location every summer. We all started praying but without a result. I spent time traveling around the Warsaw area, trying to find a suitable place, but to no avail.

When you pray for a year, two years, or five years, the excitement can start to wane. You can become discouraged, wondering if your prayers are doing anything or if you should give up.

Honestly, I stopped exploring every opportunity like I did in the first few years. There may have been some lack of faith, but it was more of a decision to forget about finding land and instead focus on doing the work of the ministry.

Looking back, I believe that there was a reason God had us wait and that his timing was perfect. The ten years of wandering in the desert before finding our "promised land" allowed us to settle in, develop our skills, build our team, and, more importantly, build our faith.

But if you had asked me back then, I wouldn't have said any of that. I would have told you I was tired of waiting and that we needed a camp now. If I had been honest, I might have confessed that I was no longer confident God was ever going to provide us with our own camp.

Boy, was I wrong.

chapter four

Our Promised Land

P roem's story is one of miracles, and our camp may be one of the best examples. But to tell you about that, I need to go back to one thousand unanswered letters and one unexpected phone call.

Proem's Camp Ministry: A Miraculous Invitation

In 1994, Proem had a few partners, but we needed more. We were looking for relationships, not just churches who would send money or mission teams.

That's still true today. Because of the size of our ministry, people assume we must have hundreds of partners. In reality, we have about twelve. We are still seeking more and praying for deep relationships with our partners.

My wife and I found ourselves in Columbus, Ohio, in 1994 because of relationships we had established with a few pastors from our time at the Word of Life Bible Institute. Needing more partners, I decided to reach out to churches around Columbus—one *thousand* churches. Yes, I sent letters to one thousand churches asking for meetings so I could share what Proem was trying to do.

While we waited for responses, I tried to earn money by doing odd jobs. I didn't make much. We lived near a pizza place and discovered they would sell us leftover pizza at the end of the night.

It wasn't what we imagined. Because of all the letters I sent out, we had assumed I would be in constant meetings and speaking at churches every Sunday for a year.

We did not get a single response from those letters.

Not one.

I was so disappointed, but God's ways are not our ways; his thoughts are higher than ours, and he had a plan.

One day in early January, I got a phone call. The voice on the other end said she was from Southeast Christian Church and invited us to attend a mission weekend in late January.

Was that because of a letter I sent them?

No.

I didn't send them a letter because I had never heard of Southeast Christian Church.

That did not keep me from saying yes. I didn't ask questions. (No, "Who are you?" No, "How did you hear about us?" No, "Could you tell me about your church?") I didn't hesitate. I just said yes.

The hundreds of meetings I expected would not happen, but there would be *one*. Just one.

At the end of January, we drove to Louisville, Kentucky, and looked for a small country church. We couldn't find it. We knew the name of the road and kept driving up and down it, but no small Southeast Christian Church. Finally, we took note of a *huge* building on a sprawling campus that we had driven past several times. I pulled into the parking lot, wondering if this could possibly be a church.

I left Ewa and Przemek in the car as I ran in to ask what exactly this was and to explain that I was looking for a church to hold a missions conference. The lady inside assured me I was in the right place and said, "Maui, we've been waiting for you. Come in!"

That weekend changed everything for Proem.

We attended the conference, and I met Bob Russell, the founding (and at that time senior) pastor of Southeast. He invited me to join him at the men's Bible study he led the next morning. I agreed and showed up, expecting to see a dozen guys sitting around a table. I walked in and saw more than one thousand men.

Bob let me know he was giving me five minutes to speak about Proem.

Wow! I had sent a thousand letters, but now, over a thousand people were ready to hear me share the vision of Proem.

One of the men listening to me that morning was Stan Franczek. Stan has been an incredible difference-maker for Proem and serves today as the president of our board.

Jim Burgen, then the youth pastor at Southeast, asked me if I'd like to preach on Sunday morning at youth church. I expected an unruly small group of grammar school-age kids, but I walked into an amazing group of over 1,500 teenagers.

On Monday, I was sitting with John Foster, the chairman of the elders of the church. He wanted to hear more about Proem. I shared our vision. We were only three years old and pretty small, but I tried to make our vision sound as big and exciting as it was in my heart.

John spoke with such a heavy southern accent I could barely understand him, but I eventually understood he was saying, "Maui, you're doing fine. You're doing fine." I thanked him, and he continued, "We'd like to come to Poland to see what you're doing." I nodded and told him I would be heading back to Poland in May.

John cut me off with a "No," then reached into his pocket and pulled out a small calendar. He consulted it and asked, "How about the end of February?" I felt like my head was spinning, but I agreed.

Three weeks later, my wife and I met three of Southeast's elders and their wives at the Cincinnati airport and flew together to Poland. Jim and Claudette Patton, who were church members, were with them as well. They were some of the first people we met at Southeast and became crucial in getting groups from Southeast to come to serve alongside us.

I was certain the entire trip was a disaster. It was frigid weather. Snow covered everything. Our team was preparing for our winter camp, but there were no activities happening for us to show our guests.

We went back to the States, feeling dejected, but when we met with John, he surprised us by saying, "We would like to be involved with your ministry. What would you like us to do?" I took a deep breath and asked if they might send a team of ten people to help with our camp in the summer. John came back with, "How about forty?"

Forty?!

I quickly agreed.

John continued, "Can you use some music?"

Music has always been a big part of our camps, so, "Yes," I told him, "We could use a few musicians to play at our camp." John replied, "No. We'll send a band for a concert." I nodded yes, not sure what he meant. That summer, the major Christian band Audio Adrenaline made its first trip to Poland. Not only did they play at camp, but we also had them do concerts at Polish military bases and a rock music festival.

God leading Southeast to notice us, invite us, and partner with us was an amazing miracle. It was a miracle that affected our ministry far beyond that first year.

I'll share more, but first, I need to take you back to years earlier.

Camp Miracles

We weren't sure anyone would show up.

When we launched our new "parachurch organization" in 1990, we needed an anchor ministry. I had experience with camps, so they felt like a natural starting point.

Our first try was with a two-week camp. We weren't sure if anyone would trust us with their kids for two weeks, and we were *stunned* when 160 campers signed up.

We then added a winter camp, which drew another hundred campers.

The camp ministry was an immediate success. We had more applications than space. We decided to offer two camps the following summer, each two weeks long. We doubled the number of campers and, more importantly, the number of decisions for the Lord. There's nothing better. When you see young people choosing to follow Jesus with their whole lives in front of them, it's worth all the effort, money, time, and prayers it took to make it happen.

The following year, we added camps for younger children, from seven to eleven years old. Because of space issues, our only option was to do the camps simultaneously. We offered two back-to-back, two-week camps for teenagers and, at the same time, two back-to-back two-week camps for younger children at a different location.

Each year, we had to find places to rent to hold the camps, clean those locations, prepare them for hosting camps for the four weeks, and then run the camps. Honestly, it was an exhausting process, but something we happily did again and again.

We soon changed our camps from two weeks long to one so we could accommodate twice the number of campers.

We started a tradition of throwing an appreciation event each summer after the camps. Every year, we would have twenty to thirty people celebrating at the Kentucky Fried Chicken in Warsaw.

We knew the camp ministry and the impact we were having on kids could keep growing *if* we had our own facility. Summer vacation from school was ten weeks long and if we had our own land, we could offer ten weeks of camp.

We started searching in the Warsaw area and, as I shared previously, found nothing that could work—for ten years.

It felt like God wasn't answering our prayers, but he was working in the shadows.

I was still working as a youth pastor and one evening a young, skinny, very quiet young man walked into our youth meeting. He hadn't been invited. He was just walking by, saw lights on, and decided to come in. I greeted him, gave him a Bible, and offered to pray for him.

Eventually, that young man went to seminary. When he graduated, he moved from Warsaw to Tomaszów Mazowiecki to be involved in a church plant, the process of starting a new congregation. In Tomaszów Mazowiecki, he saw an ad in the local newspaper for a fifteen-acre camp for sale in the nearby village of Zakościele. He remembered that we had been searching for a place to purchase and called me to ask if we were still looking.

I decided to check it out.

It was winter and the place was in total disrepair. Everything was overgrown. I later learned the owner, a large textile company, went bankrupt at the beginning of the 1990s. The place sat empty for seven years before it was finally put up for sale by the bank.

Despite the condition, I looked at the camp through eyes of faith and thought it could be the Promised Land for which we had been searching.

Then I found out the price: US $1.5 million.

It was way too much. I was heartbroken. I prayed, "God, why did you lead us here? It's so far out of our reach. There's no way. It's too expensive."

We didn't make a bid.

But neither did anyone else.

A year later, the price went down due to a lack of interest.

I talked to a representative of the bank that had taken ownership of the land to see if we could rent it. They weren't interested.

So, we didn't make a bid. But neither did anyone else.

The following year, the price went down to $300,000.

Whoa.

We didn't have $300,000, but the amount at least seemed reachable. We had the down payment of $30,000 and trusted that if God wanted us to have this land, he would allow us to raise the other $270,000.

Our bid and down payment were accepted. However, there was a risk. If we couldn't raise the remaining $270,000, we would lose our $30,000. When we gave the money, we were told we had thirty days to pay the remaining $270,000.

Gulp.

We started asking God and our supporters for help raising the money. Soon, we had raised about $40,000. We still had $230,000 to go.

People from Southeast Christian Church came and gave us a check for $100,000. (Remember I told you the miracle God gave us in introducing us to Southeast was a gift that kept on giving?) We all rejoiced as we had never received—never even seen!—such a big check.

We still had $130,000 to go.

A few small gifts trickled in, but the due date for the remaining $270,000 was fast approaching, and we realized we would not have all the money we needed.

I was in a train station when my cell phone started ringing. I answered, and Matt Chalfant from Southeast asked, "Maui, are you sitting or standing?" When someone asks you that, you need to sit down.

I sat down.

Matt continued, "If we were to give you all the money you need to purchase this space, Could you use the $140,000 you've raised so far for the renovation of the camp?"

Long silence.

Just to be sure, I asked, "Let me repeat this to see if I understood you correctly. You are saying Southeast is willing to pay all the $300,000 if we use the $140,000 for renovations."

I held my breath.

"Yes," Matt answered, "that is what I meant."

I blurted out, as fast as I could: "Of course we can and will!"

I was excited to call our staff to tell them the news. I called my wife. I probably told it to total strangers in the train station.

Days later, Southeast wired the money, we paid the remaining balance, and the camp was ours.

Renovation Miracles

We had the camp, and it was time to renovate. It was winter, but we had to get started so we could be ready for our summer camps. We prayed for guidance because we didn't have expertise in doing renovations.

God responded to our prayers by leading a supporter of our ministry to hire forty people to do the work.

There was a lot of work to do. The place was ugly and needed new wiring, plumbing, and insulation. We had a crew who did plastering after the electricians and plumbers were done and another that did tiling and other finishing touches after the plastering crew was done.

We expanded the "hotel" and doubled the size of the dining room. We upgraded the resident cabins.

When we bought the camp, there was no "magazyn," the L-shaped building currently used for main sessions and other multimedia events. There were few meeting rooms and no room big enough for a large group to meet in when it was too cold to gather outside.

We were praying about how we could have a space big enough for the main sessions of the camps when I noticed a kid who was registered for the camp was the child of a laborer for a tent-making company. I went to the business and asked if they had a used tent we could purchase for a meeting space. The owner apologized as they only sold new tents. He asked if we'd be interested in a new tent, but the price was out of our reach. I asked, "Are you sure you can't sell us a used tent?" "It's never happened," he replied, "but who knows, maybe it will."

Persistent, I called two days later, "Sir, we need it so badly. Please reconsider." The owner told me, "Come back tomorrow."

The next day, he showed me the tent they were using to cover the area where he produced the other tents. He graciously told me he could sell us that used tent for a reasonable price.

I was elated.

He gave me the measurements of the tent and said, "Put in the foots." I didn't know what he meant. He explained, "It's the concrete we put the posts in. Put in the foots and I'll come and install this tent."

A crew of volunteers put in the footings.

The day before the man was supposed to come to install the tent, he called me, "Something has happened. I'll come see you tomorrow, but we've got some problems here."

We only had two weeks until camps started and needed the tent. We didn't have time for problems.

The man showed up the next day with a brand-new tent. I felt distraught and reminded him we didn't have enough money to buy one.

He smiled. "I'm not asking you for additional money. When I gave you the measurements for the foots, I told you it was five meters, but it turns out my old tent was four meters. Since it was my mistake, I decided to give you a new tent for half the price of the old tent. I came myself because I wanted to surprise you and see your face."

He saw my face, which was beaming with a huge, grateful smile because God had provided another miracle.

That new tent, which served as our first meeting place, is still in good shape today, twenty-three years later.

We had our tent but needed a stable floor underneath. How do you think that happened? Southeast sent a group of men, including Stan Franczek, to help with the renovations, and they put in the floor.

Now, we needed a place for people to sit. We figured we'd put in benches, but someone suggested we try to find a store that would sell us two hundred chairs at an affordable price. A few days before the camp was to start, Ewa and I went to IKEA to check on the price of chairs. We found five folding metal chairs on sale for half the regular price. I asked a store employee if they had more than five. She said she would go check and came back asking, "How many do you need?" "We need two hundred," we told her. She said, "You're in luck. There are 220 of those chairs." We asked how long the sale on the chairs would last, and she said, "Until Sunday." We went the next day and purchased two hundred chairs. Out of curiosity, I went back to IKEA on Monday to check the price of the remaining twenty chairs. They were double the price of the two hundred we purchased! Yet another miracle!

Just a few days before camp was scheduled to begin, we didn't have a tent, a floor, or chairs for the campers to sit in. But we got it all—in God's perfect timing—just in time.

In the book of Nehemiah, we see the Israelites go to work rebuilding the wall around Jerusalem. They complete the work in only fifty-two days.

In Zakościele, Poland, forty workers (and occasionally some volunteers) worked from early January to the end of June. The winter was so mild they didn't lose a day due to weather. They completed the work on June 24. We quickly set up the furniture and beds, and the next day, on June 25, two hundred teenagers arrived at our very first week of camp on our own Promised Land property.

Expansion And The Future

Now that we had our own property that could house two hundred kids, we began thinking about adding more camps.

The first camp we added was Fishart, an arts camp.

Because of our connections with Americans, the next was an English-language camp.

Soon we added sports camps.

We also realized we could now host conferences.

We offered a weekend women's conference in early May. There was so much interest, we doubled it the following year.

At the second women's conference, the ladies said, "Why don't you do something for our husbands?" We doubted men would come for something like that, but the women said, "We'll make sure they come," so we began having men's weekends.

We also started doing weekend conferences during the winter break when school is out.

The property gave us so many opportunities to reach the community.

We also launched leadership development weekends at the camp. Most of these are for our staff or partners, but we want to make them available for leaders of other ministries.

Christian Camping International—a worldwide organization we belong to and of which our nephew Daniel Wawrzyniak is now president of the Polish chapter—held trainings at our camp until COVID-19 and the war in Ukraine stopped it. In fact, those trainings allowed us to build relationships with Ukrainians, which led to our camp being a refugee center during the war. You'll read more about that later.

Our facility is also used for retreats and gatherings of missionaries by other ministries and churches, like one of our largest supporting churches, Compassion Christian Church from Savannah, Georgia.

We have also hosted meetings of educators from the Association of Christian Schools International and Eureka.

In more recent years, we began producing *Road to Jerusalem* at the campground.

Currently, we're praying about—and have a blueprint for—a new building to add to our camp—the Leadership and Development Center. With all that's going on, we could use the space! As of this writing, we have part of the funds raised and are waiting for a permit from city hall. Our plan is to build a facility with twelve apartments, each with two bedrooms, a living room, and a kitchen, so that Christian leaders from all over Poland and Europe can come with their families to develop additional preaching, teaching, and leadership skills. Those rooms could be used by those coming for a weekend, but also for those planning a longer stay with us, like a pastor on sabbatical. When completed, the Leadership and Development Center will be at the main entrance of the camp, with a nice reception area and a big parking lot in front of the building.

It's a crazy dream, but we have learned we cannot outdream God. He has met every need we have, and when we look back at Proem's history, we see a trail of miracles.

chapter five

OPEN DOORS

When people used to ask me what they could pray for Proem, I would say, "Open doors. Pray that God gives us open doors."

After all, Paul asked the believers in Colossae to pray "that God may open a door for our message, so that we may proclaim the mystery of Christ" (Colossians 4:3) and celebrated when God opened doors (see Acts 14:27).

It's a great prayer, but I don't ask for that anymore.

Why?

Because God has already answered that prayer. The doors are wide open for us. Now, we pray for people to walk through them.

There is almost unlimited opportunity in our country. We have open doors, and one of the best examples of that is our music ministry.

Proem's Music Ministry: The Birth Of Exodus 15

I wrote earlier that we chose camps to be our anchor ministry. It's how we launched Proem, and it's no exaggeration that nearly everything we do today is rooted in the camps' ministry, definitely including our music ministry.

Eventually, we put on music camps, but one of the most prominent parts of every camp, regardless of the focus of the week, is the worship time.

God has blessed us with incredible singers, musicians, and tech people, so we've always had top-tier quality. We have strategically chosen music styles for the age group the week of camp is targeting. At first, music was just part of what we did for camps, but gradually, it took on a life of its own.

On the first night of each week of camp, the rules are presented in a humorous montage of musical skits. The kids look forward to it, and though the humor draws them in, they're absorbing the rules as well. It's not uncommon to hear campers sing rules to each other when they see other campers breaking the rules.

Our music ministry was taken up a level in 2005 when Exodus 15 was officially formed as a worship band. The name of the band comes from Moses's song in Exodus 15. After God saved the Israelites from the Egyptian army by allowing them to cross the Red Sea on dry ground, Moses and Miriam led them in worship with lyrics like:

[1] "I will sing to the Lord,
for he is highly exalted.

Both horse and driver
he has hurled into the sea.

[2] "The Lord is my strength and my defense;
he has become my salvation....

[13] "In your unfailing love you will lead
the people you have redeemed.

In your strength you will guide them
to your holy dwelling....

[18] "The Lord reigns
for ever and ever."

The song is about worshipping God in gratitude for his miracles in our lives, which is the heart of the message our band shares.

Doors Open

As Exodus 15 became an official band, they expanded their reach beyond camps, and their influence grew slowly but surely every year.

They went to a studio and recorded their music so we could have it to give out.

Soon, requests started coming in for the band to travel and give concerts outside of camps. Honestly, I was not excited about the idea because they were working for Proem, and this would take them away. But the band was passionate about affecting people through their music, and I knew God had opened this door for them. We prayed for wisdom and had very intentional conversations about how many concerts they could do each year and how to calendar it so they were available when we needed them in Zakościele. We met at a coffee bar, and I laid out the situation, "We have fifty-two weeks a year. We must set aside two months in the summer. That means we can't have more than thirty to thirty-five concerts a year."

Invitations kept coming in—more than thirty-five requests a year—some for concerts and many from churches. Most were evangelical churches, but some were Catholic.

At the time, we only had our camp equipment, so we began sharing with our partners the door God had opened for our music ministry. Soon, the first substantial donation for equipment came in, which we took as a sign from God that we were moving in the right direction. Because of God and the hard work of Przemek (our soundman) and Majkel (our drummer and manager), we pretty quickly had the necessary sound and light systems, musical instruments, and microphones.

The invitations keep coming—our band has been invited to play in America, Belgium, and Lithuania, along with Michael W. Smith in Poland at the Festival of Hope.

The band can sing and share their testimonies in Polish and English.

Exodus 15 has now recorded ten albums and one DVD, with another DVD in production as I write this book.

One of the funny stories that came out of filming the first DVD is that Tomek Gużda, our "lights guy," had to leave the country for an emergency, so we asked an intern to step in for him and run the lights for the worship experiences we filmed. He did a phenomenal job, and no one knew until afterward that he was colorblind. (Perhaps that's another miracle!)

At that time, we were pretty involved in Afghanistan, and we used part of the money we raised with the sale of the videos to support the ministry that was happening there.

So many people—especially children—wanted to meet the band members that we started offering "Meet Exodus 15" events.

I may be biased, but as far as I'm concerned, they are the best.

Catholic Doors

Some Catholics in Poland still think of non-Catholic churches as a cult. Many who consider themselves Catholic in Poland do not even attend church and don't have a genuine faith in or relationship with the Lord. For years, we have prayed that God would open doors for us to share the Gospel with them.

He has—through Exodus 15.

Catholic churches started asking Exodus 15 to lead worship at their family retreats. The band leads the music and shares testimonies about having a life-changing relationship with God.

A few years ago, they were invited to sing at a rally organized by the Catholic Church and held at the national soccer stadium in Warsaw. Exodus 15 gave a one-hour worship concert for the forty thousand young people in the stadium.

Then, they were invited to play for a huge youth rally when the Pope was visiting Kraków. About two thousand young people filled the old town square. Two Catholic priests introduced Exodus 15. After the concert, the priests were supposed to share the Word of God, but one of them told our band, "Keep worshipping. Then, you share the Gospel. Share your testimonies and invite people to receive Jesus as their Lord and Savior."

I sat and watched with a full heart as Agata, Karolina, and Estera, the singers of Exodus 15, told their testimonies, explained why Jesus had to die and that he died for everyone, and prayed for those who wanted to receive Jesus.

Exodus 15 helps Catholics to see Jesus and to see that non-Catholic Christians are not members of a cult but followers of Jesus.

God May Open A Door

I confessed that I was not originally enthusiastic about sending our band out. I have come around. It's become an exceptional way of spreading the word about Proem and, more importantly, about Jesus.

Sharing Jesus through song has a way of opening minds and speaking to people's hearts.

It opens doors.

I pray God continues opening these doors and that we are always ready to step through them so that we may proclaim the mystery of Christ.

I also pray for you that God will open wide doors for you to do effective work for him (see 1 Corinthians 16:9). That you will pray for, keep watch for, and be ready to run through whatever doors God opens for you to share Jesus.

chapter six

A DRASTIC CHANGE

Pawel and Asia are a typical husband and wife you might meet in Poland.

They consider themselves Catholic but don't go to church. In Poland, 90 percent identify as Catholic, but less than 40 percent attend church services.

Pawel and Asia would say they believe in Jesus, but their faith is more like their parents' or the tradition of their country. They might admit their faith is unimportant to them, and it certainly does not affect their lives in any way.

Pawel is an alcoholic. He may realize it, but it's easy to justify because so many Polish men drink heavily on a daily basis. His drinking negatively affects his family. Asia hates it but believes there's nothing that can be done about it.

Pawel and Asia have two kids who will almost certainly follow in their footsteps.

We started Proem with a mission to reach people like Pawel and Asia with the Gospel of Jesus. How could we introduce people to God's life-transforming, eternity-changing grace?

Eventually, we began planting churches to reach the Pawels and Asias. But I'll be honest, that's not why we started our first church. When we started our first church, we didn't even think we were starting a church! Honestly, it was never part of our plan.

Starting A Church—By Mistake

When we purchased the land in Zakościele for our camp, our staff all lived in Warsaw. Realizing our ministry would revolve around the camp, they packed up their lives and moved to live—at least temporarily—at the camp. Some settled in Tomaszów Mazowiecki, a town near Zakościele.

For several months we all commuted the hundred kilometers to Warsaw every Sunday morning for church. It was not ideal, but there weren't great options. The only non-Catholic church in the area was a Lutheran church in Tomaszów Mazowiecki, but it didn't seem to have any spiritual life. The young man who had come to our youth meeting and told us about the property for our camp had moved to Tomaszów Mazowiecki to start a church, but it didn't survive.

Eventually, partly because we didn't want to continue making the drive every week or be part of a church so far from where we live, we started meeting together in Tomaszów Mazowiecki. We had rented a small new building—originally built to be an appliances shop—to use as an internet café and a preschool. Every Sunday morning, twelve or fourteen of us—just the Proem staff—would meet in that space to worship God together.

Soon, other people became curious about who we were and what we were doing on Sunday mornings. Some were parents of the kids in our preschool or in our language school.

Our church—which we didn't originally think of as a church—was growing slowly. We were not trying to grow our attendance; we were building relationships and serving the people around us. Through that, God kept adding people.

At the same time, people from the United States kept coming to help us serve our community.

We now had thirty to forty people each Sunday, and our meeting space was getting too small. We didn't know what to do, so we prayed for a place to meet.

There was an old movie theater that closed in 2001 when a more modern theater opened. We met with the owner and suggested, "You don't use this building. Maybe you would like to sell it to us?" He told us it was not for sale, only for rent. We turned him down.

A few months later, he called and asked me to make an offer to buy the theater. We had almost no money, so I made an extremely low offer. He balked, "No, that's too small of a price."

Six months later, he called again and asked if we were still interested. I told him we were, but still could only pay the price I had offered previously. He rejected our offer again.

A couple of months later, he showed up at my office and offered us a five-year lease. I politely rejected his proposal. "We're only interested if we can buy it."

He called me several days later, "OK, I will sell it to you."

The location of the theater was excellent, including the wonderful address of "1 Jerusalem Street."

We started the renovations, which cost three times as much as we paid to purchase the building. We wouldn't have had the money to do the necessary work except that, again, Southeast Christian Church stepped up with a big donation. We also had some other donors pitch in to help make our new church home a reality. It was 2008 when we finally finished the renovation and moved in.

Before our first Sunday, we went to the building and prayed for God's blessing. Up to that point, we had maybe forty people joining us on Sunday mornings, so we set up fifty chairs. We celebrated. "Yes, we have arrived! We will be good for the next ten years!"

By the next year, we had one hundred people gathering on Sunday mornings. People were coming and being saved. In the second year, we had to add a second service. After a while, even two services were not enough.

God's Plan

Looking back, we didn't plan on starting a church, but I believe it was part of God's plan.

In one sense, adding a church to our ministry was a drastic change, but in another way, it didn't feel like a change at all. Why?

From the beginning, Proem has been about sharing the Gospel and introducing people to a saving faith in and relationship with Jesus so we can affect their lives and eternities.

How do we do that?

In the beginning, it was almost exclusively through camps. Then, it was through our music ministry. Then, to our surprise, we started a church. Today, we also use our school and counseling center and various other ways to proclaim his name.

It really doesn't matter *how* we share Jesus as long as we are sharing Jesus. There are many ways, some more effective at certain times than others. In some sense, we want to share Jesus in all the different ways we can, as long as we can do so effectively. We want everyone to know Jesus.

That's God's plan. God "wants all people to be saved and to come to a knowledge of the truth" (1 Timothy 2:4). He is "not wanting anyone to perish, but everyone to come to repentance" (2 Peter 3:9).

God's plan for *accomplishing his plan is us—you* and me. I've heard it said that we are God's plan A, and there is no plan B. God wants to use us to help everyone know Jesus. At Proem, we will do whatever it takes, even if it's starting a church, which was never part of our plan.

On To Łódź

Much like Tomaszów Mazowiecki, starting a second church in Łódź was not our original intention.

There are four million people living within one hundred kilometers of our camp at Zakościele. Other than Warsaw, the largest city in Poland is Łódź, with a population of about one million people but no more than five hundred evangelical believers in a handful of tiny churches.

Łódź's demographics are interesting. It was built mostly during the textile boom in the eighteenth century. Many companies located there because of a tax exemption granted to businesses that invested in the textile industry.

Łódź (pronounced wootch) means "boat" in Polish. Though there are no rivers today, back in the 1800s, sixteen or seventeen rivers crisscrossed through the city. The rivers were vital because water was needed to produce fabric, but the industry basically dried up all the rivers.

In the 1940s, when the Nazis started moving Jews to the ghettos, the first was in Łódź. Today, the biggest cemetery—with 300,000 graves—for Jewish people from all of Europe is in Łódź.

During Communism, Łódź was still primarily a textile city, but artistic schools also emerged. Today, there are prestigious art and film academies in Łódź.

Because Łódź was not destroyed during the war, it's often used as a location for making films. Some people even call the city "Hollyłódź."

I mentioned that about 40 percent of Poles attend church. In Łódź, that number is less than 20 percent, and almost everyone who does attends Catholic churches. We started driving there to do prayer walks because there were so few Christians in the city (Jesus would say it is "white for harvest"). We also had Exodus 15 perform concerts once a month. Then, we began doing "serve the city" projects. And then, yes, we started another church.

On one visit, we found the "Maui Theater." No, it is not named after me. Remember, "Maui" means little. We rented the theater and held Sunday morning gatherings there. It's now years later, and we have found the spiritual soil in Łódź very difficult, but still, we have more than a hundred people attending church in Łódź every Sunday morning.

On To Piotrków

From Łódź, we decided to go to Piotrków, which means "Peter's city."

Piotrków is fairly close to Tomaszów Mazowiecki, but it is much older— Piotrków was established in the twelfth century while Tomaszów Mazowiecki was founded in the nineteenth century—and it has 10,000 more people.

When we decided to target Piotrków, we knew the right approach was to not just repeat what we had done in the past. We needed to understand what was unique about Piotrków so we could know the best way to serve its people and the most effective way to start a church there. We have the same goal in every city; the challenge is determining the best approach. The message always stays the same, but the methods may need to change.

We look, for example, at the demographics of the city. What is the age of the people, and what are the education levels? Is there a university? Are there public concerts? What sports are important? We look at everything we can, and then determine how we can help.

As we did prayer walks and met the people, we discovered it was very different, even from nearby Tomaszów Mazowiecki.

In Tomaszów Mazowiecki and Łódź, we found there was a need for coffee shops and preschools so we could start one, meet people's needs, and build relationships with them. But in Piotrków there were plenty of coffee shops and preschools, so we realized our old method wouldn't work. We noticed areas requiring renovation and that parents needed after-school help for their kids and knew that teaching English is always welcomed. So, we went to the city hall and asked if we could start doing "serve the city" projects. They agreed, and we got to work.

Several families from the United States and one Polish family moved to Piotrków, and we now meet for church services once a month and Bible study every Wednesday. Those Bible studies and church services usually have about twenty-five people in attendance. We're praying that we'll start meeting every Sunday in 2024.

And On We Go

When we had just one church in Tomaszów Mazowiecki, we set a goal of starting five churches by 2030. Today, we have two fully started, one in process, and two more to go.

Our current thinking is not to go too far from Tomaszów Mazowiecki since that's where most of our staff is located. We're looking at cities about fifty miles or less from our hub. We go to these cities, do prayer walks, study the demographics, and ask God if it's a place where he wants us to establish a presence.

When Poland became a democracy, many church-planting organizations flooded our country, thinking they could be successful and fill Poland with evangelical churches in just a few years. It didn't work, I think, because they didn't seek to understand the culture. Eventually, they withdrew their missionaries and closed their churches.

One feature of our country they failed to understand is how strong the pull of the Catholic tradition is here. If you ask a Polish person on the street, "Are you a Christian?" they will answer, "Of course, I'm a Catholic." But if you then ask them if they have a relationship with God, they'll say, "You must be in a cult. What do you want from me?" When I tell people my parents and grandparents were Polish, born in our country, and were evangelical Christians, they scoff, "That's impossible."

I shared the parable of the sower with you. Well, Poland has a lot of hard soil. It is not an easy place to share the Gospel or start a church. Most people believe in God—which can keep them from thinking they need anything more. They believe in God, but a distant God who has nothing to do with their lives or with our world today.

It's not easy to do evangelism in this place, but we know it's our mission and that all things are possible with our God. We know we need to keep doing it because people need Jesus. We keep doing it because of the Pawels and Asias.

Asia And Pawel

Remember, Asia and Pawel thought of themselves as Catholics but didn't go to church. Pawel was an alcoholic, and his drinking was negatively affecting his family.

Then, the daughter started attending Proem's after-school program in Tomaszów Mazowiecki. Every month, the whole family went to our monthly "Kidstuff" program.

Asia saw an opportunity for Pawel's life to change, so she signed him up for Proem's men's kayaking weekend. He didn't go. Six months later, she signed him up again. This time, he agreed.

Pawel discovered the weekend had three rules: no swearing, no drinking, and no complaining. As an alcoholic, it was extremely difficult to go a couple of days without drinking, but even still, it was an incredible experience.

The twenty other men were all different—a policeman, a former priest, even a fan of a rival soccer club. The one thing they had in common was their relationships with God. Conversations about God came easily to them. Pawel had never heard anyone talk like that about God. He says, "During the three days of kayaking, I had many conversations about God with one of the pastors, Adam Pańczak. He told me my life would never be the same. It didn't mean much at the time."

The next week, Pawel and Asia went to their first church service. They intentionally left their kids at home, not knowing what to expect at the church.

That day, they were introduced to Grzegorz and Gosia, who hosted a Bible study for married couples at their house. Pawel and Asia started attending and felt like they met God in that group.

Asia became certain she wanted to follow Jesus and got baptized. Pawel, however, stopped going to church. He was drinking more and more and didn't want anyone to know or to ask him about it. The few times Asia talked him into going, he would put on his coat and leave immediately when the service ended.

A few months later, there was a church retreat in Zakościele. Pawel thought that since his wife had been baptized and it seemed to help her, he should get baptized as well. He got baptized and promised himself he would stop drinking, thinking, "If I break this promise, there's something wrong with me."

After the retreat, Pawel went to celebrate his baptism with his brother-in-law and found himself drinking with him. He felt convicted and like he had to call Adam. He asked Adam about a Christian rehab center Adam had mentioned, and soon he was signed up to go.

Pawel went to rehab for six months and came home a new man. He says he became more aware of and understood the implications of his salvation. Asia says he returned completely different. He was now asking questions about her and the kids' lives. He seemed to care and worry about them. He repeatedly told them, "I love you," words they had almost never heard.

Asia calls it a "drastic change" and affirms that the change is still holding true today.

Pawel says, "I learned that God is love and that I can do everything in love."

Asia and Pawel both ended up working at the school, and Pawel drove the bus.

They say, "The church and Proem became a huge part of our lives. If I were to wake up tomorrow and the church would be gone, it would be like we lost everything that is most important to us. Our entire lives center on the church and God. We met God at the church through Proem."

That's why we start churches.

chapter seven

SEE A NEED— MEET A NEED

I told you how, when we were in Bible school in America, we memorized Bible verses. I loved it, *except* I had to memorize them in English. That was not easy.

I have not yet shared my favorite Bible verse. I love Psalm 32:8, "I will instruct you and teach you in the way you should go; I will counsel you with my loving eye on you." God promises that he is always watching and will lead us.

Our strategy at Proem is "See a need—meet a need."

We believe that God has called his people to meet the needs of others. Jesus did and taught that time and time again. In Jeremiah, we learn that we are to "seek the peace and prosperity of the city to which I have carried you into exile. Pray to the Lord for it, because if it prospers, you too will prosper" (Jeremiah 29:7). And James tells us, "Religion that God our Father accepts as pure and faultless is this: to look after orphans and widows in their distress" (James 1:27).

We love our communities by serving them, which opens them up to hearing the Gospel. And how do we find needs we can meet? God instructs us and teaches us in the way we should go.

The Seeds Of Meeting Needs

At the beginning of Proem—before we had even named ourselves Proem—we were running camps for kids. Was that because God commands us in the Bible to do camps? No. We did camps because camps were needed. Young people needed a productive and positive place to go during their summer break from school, and parents appreciated it.

We began looking to use sports to meet needs and build relationships with young people. Back when we didn't have anything but camps, I went to the dimly lit office of the Polish version of *Sports Illustrated*. It was a small, black-and-white magazine about recreation. I approached the editor—a small, serious man with a somber look on his face—with an idea. "I like your magazine. You talk about physical recreation and using your body to achieve your goals. But there's a weakness because a person is more than just a body." He nodded as if he recognized that was true. I continued, "Since you're writing about how to be better physically, would you want me to address people's spiritual well-being? Some athletes are into holistic training. The mind, body, soul, and spirit go hand in hand." I offered to write stories using illustrations from Sports Spectrum magazine—a publication in the States for sports fans who are followers of Jesus or desire to learn more. He was noncommittal, so I left the office disappointed. But a couple weeks later, he called and came to our office to talk. Zaba, my secretary at the time, was so nervous about his visit that she spilled coffee all over his lap. Maybe that's why he offered me four pages in his magazine! I wrote articles every month for two years. Later, from 1995–2000, we created and sent out our own sports magazine targeted at young people.

Sports are extremely popular in Poland, but one that did not have a big following was baseball. When we were in the United States in 1994, Przemek was twelve, and someone gave him a glove and ball. He really took to the sport, but when we returned to Poland, he could only toss a ball by himself in our backyard. We looked for a team he could join, but there weren't any. That led us to realize there might be a need we could meet. We organized a group of parents in our neighborhood and founded a baseball little league. We then signed up with Little League Baseball in Williamsport, Pennsylvania. Baseball was so new in Poland there was no place to purchase equipment, so I sent a message to Little League Baseball and the American Embassy in Warsaw. Soon, America sent baseball equipment to the embassy. Guess who brought it to us? Former US President George H. W. Bush! And guess who he brought with him? Hall of Fame baseball legend Stan Musial (who was of Polish descent)! The President of Little League Baseball in Williamsport came with them. They did some training with our young players.

Sometimes, as you try to meet your needs, God does some crazy cool things.

In those early days, we just kept trying to meet our needs.

Instead of just going out on the streets and preaching the Gospel to strangers, we created spaces for people outside the church to meet and for us to meet people outside the church. We rented spaces in restaurants, tea houses, and coffee shops. We held movie nights where people could discuss films after watching them. I told you how we brought in chiropractors and staged basketball tournaments.

Why? Because those were real needs we could meet. By doing so, we earned people's trust and the right to be heard.

How We Start Churches

In the last chapter, I shared with you our journey into starting churches. I didn't tell you *how* we started churches, but by now, you can probably guess. We see a need and meet a need.

The process is not a quick one. It is slow and deliberate and takes patient partners. Near the beginning of our ministry, the pastor of Mount Pleasant Christian Church in Greenwood, Indiana, asked Guy Quinette to lead a trip to Proem for basketball camp. Mount Pleasant is committed to church planting, and their passion was contagious. Now, thirty mission trips later, this incredible church continues to bless us in so many ways.

I shared how we, by mistake, started a church in Tomaszów Mazowiecki as our staff gathered on Sunday mornings to worship God together. But *where* were we meeting? When our staff relocated from Warsaw, we immediately began looking for needs in Tomaszów Mazowiecki. We saw that people in that city needed a connecting place, so we opened a coffee shop.

The internet was just becoming popular, but most people did not have access to it. A need! So, at the coffee shop, we opened an internet café where people could sign up to use one of the three refurbished computers for thirty minutes. There were *long* lines.

Young mothers were coming to the coffee shop and internet café with small children. Another need! We began offering childcare. Moms appreciated it so much; in the next few years, we opened a preschool. In the beginning, we had twenty-five kids from nine in the morning until two in the afternoon. We discovered there was a need for people to have their kids watched in the afternoons, so we expanded our hours. The second year, we added another age group and another each following year.

The space we rented served as the location of our original fledgling Proem staff church, and people we met through the coffee shop, internet café, and nursery were most of the first people who joined us.

Later, after we purchased the movie theater and were more established as a church, we continued to seek needs we could meet.

We began Kontact, a city-wide outreach event involving hundreds of international volunteers who share God's love in practical ways. This helped people view our church as a safe place and emboldened them to show up.

We also started what we call "the party behind the gate," which Americans would call a "block party." We threw fun parties in poor neighborhoods that helped us to meet our neighbors and led naturally to lifestyle evangelism.

God pointed out another unmet need as we met and served shoulder-to-shoulder with other not-for-profit organizations. We put together a booklet listing the names and phone numbers of organizations serving our city. Once a year, Tomaszów Mazowiecki has a city fair at which we give away these books. Later, people from Łódź's city hall came and asked us to participate in producing a similar book for their city.

Our efforts in Tomaszów Mazowiecki have been so respected that Rafal Piekarski, the pastor of our church in Tomaszów Mazowiecki, which we call the TOMY church, was asked to be the chairperson of a city-wide nonprofit organization and later invited to work with the senator of the whole county.

I shared that after Tomaszów Mazowiecki, we started a church in Łódź. How? In exactly the same way. We looked for needs and how we could serve the city projects. Most often, we would go to the welfare department and ask how we could meet the needs of the people there in Łódź. They would give us ten to fifteen places for renovation, including apartments for single moms and orphanages, and we would go to work.

The main street of Łódź, Piotrkowska Street, is lined with hundreds of restaurants and pubs. It is thoroughly secular. In fact, at one point, it was the only street in Poland that had a gay pride parade. I asked a local artist what he thought of us starting a Christian café on Piotrkowska Street. He looked at me blankly, "What's a Christian café?" I described a coffee shop with no alcohol or smoking. He was bewildered. "That is weird. There's nothing like that in Łódź. Maybe people would walk in out of curiosity." We rented a small space and opened "PT 109," a coffee shop where our church in Łódź was conceived.

Now that we've established the new church in Łódź, we are planting in Piotrków, a city about 50 kilometers away. How? You already know the answer. We learned that there were plenty of preschools and nice coffee shops. Those were not needs. So, we went to the city hall and asked if we could carry out a "serve the city" project. We also started English classes. We learned that parents needed assistance with their children and to help them learn, so we started an after-school program for students.

To reach our goal, we must start two more churches in the next few years. Though we have some places we are considering, I don't know where we'll plant those churches, but I do know how. We will go to the city, talk to the people at city hall, do prayer walks, meet people, find out their needs, and do our best to meet them.

God Whispers

Though we do research, meet people, and observe the community, our essential strategy for reaching more people is listening for God's whisper. He puts people in front of us and shows us how we can serve them.

Wherever you are, whatever you do each day, I am convinced God will put people in your path so you can be the hands and feet of Jesus to them. I wonder if you're looking for those people and listening for God's whisper as he directs you to his children who need Jesus.

In Poland, as we contemplate how we can reach more people with the Gospel, we often look at the US and sometimes hear God whispering, "Look at what they're doing. You could do that. It would work in Poland."

We saw churches in America doing a beautiful prom-like experience for people with special needs called "Night to Shine." Knowing there are people with special needs in our communities, we decided to do our own version.

We saw churches in America doing productions of *Journey to Bethlehem* and *Road to Jerusalem* and felt God leading us to follow their example. Those events have been incredibly effective and helped us to reach more people who are without Jesus.

None of it was our idea. We followed the precedent of other churches and ministries.

Even more, we are determined to see needs and meet needs, following the instruction and teaching of our God, who promises to counsel us with his loving eye on us.

It's that commitment to meeting needs that led us to another unexpected development—starting schools.

chapter eight

METHODS CHANGE— THE MESSAGE DOESN'T

You remember the story.

Thousands have been listening to Jesus teach. Their souls are full, but their bellies are empty. Jesus, who is where we learned to "see a need, meet a need," sees people who are hungry, so he asks his disciples to feed them. The disciples are dumbfounded. They have no food and tell Jesus they will not be able to find the amount of food necessary to feed the huge crowds.

I love what Jesus does. He focuses *not* on what they *don't* have available but on what they *do*.

A boy in the crowd has a sack lunch.

How do you see a need and meet a need? You start with the need, and then you focus on *what you have*.

Proem's Education Ministry: Back In America

My wife, Ewa, is a teacher by education and profession. She worked in schools when we were first married but mostly stayed home to raise our son and help with the ministry once Przemek was born.

What did we have?

A leader who was passionate about education.

Ewa dreamt and repeatedly talked about the need for better education in Poland and the impact we could make if we had a school.

Then, when Przemek was in fifth grade, we spent a year in Columbus, Ohio. He attended a big Christian school, and everything about it was astonishing to Ewa, as it was almost the opposite of what schools were like in Poland.

Teachers were friendly to and built relationships with the students. There was an atmosphere of mutual respect. Grace was in place. If a student didn't do his homework, it was not an automatic F. The teacher would seek to understand what was happening in the student's life; why didn't they do their homework? The teachers were always encouraging, "You can do this. You did a great job. You can do better."

We loved it, and it gave Ewa a vision of what could happen in Poland.

In Poland, A School Is Born

When we returned to Poland, we were still too small to think about starting a school, but the dream was planted. It was not in our business plan, but just like starting a church, there was a need there, and when the time was right, God opened a door.

I told you how we started a preschool in Tomaszów Mazowiecki to help mothers who came to our coffee shop and internet café. At first, it was babies and then toddlers. It didn't take long before parents—who loved how we were caring for their kids—asked us to continue with an elementary school.

We established a two-hour kindergarten where kids could come and learn while their parents did their shopping. We looked around and realized there was a great need for a school that could better serve kids than the public ones run by the city.

We were offering English as a second language in our coffee shop. Alicja Zwolak-Plichta took one of our adult classes, and her kids were taking one for children. She asked, "Can I stay and hear how you teach kids?" We learned that she worked in education and dreamed of starting a school that prioritized children. When we told her about what we had experienced in America and our dream to do the same in Poland, she could barely contain herself, "It is my dream to do this kind of education!"

Later, Alicja joined us on Sunday mornings and eventually made a decision for Christ. She became dedicated to the Lord and to ministry.

As our first group of kids reached six years of age, their parents asked, "Where should we send our kid next year? Why don't you let them continue their education here?" After offering kindergarten, we added first grade, then, year by year, second, then third, fourth, and fifth.

Usually, we try to add no more than twenty students per year because we want to create a great connection between the teachers and students. Later we were able to hire more teachers and therefore enroll even more students.

Every new student was a new person we could introduce to the Lord. Even if we met with their parents only when they dropped their kids off and picked them up, there were still ten meetings a week, week after week. That's a huge connection.

I am thankful for Zaba, who provided much of the leadership as we created the education center and made Ewa's dream a reality. Not only Ewa but Alicja's too, as she later became the principal of the school. She is such a positive person and invests so much time in building relationships with the children and their parents. We are so grateful for her leadership.

Growing Pains

Parents were thrilled to see how we treated their children with love. We soon had one hundred students in our K–5 school. We were maxed out.

To continue we would need a new facility. I wanted to take it slowly; after all, it had taken us an entire decade to find land for our camp. But Zaba and my wife asked, "What will we do with these children who are finishing fifth grade?" I told them there were other schools around. Ewa asked, "Isn't this something we've dreamed about since *our* son was in fifth grade? Did we want him to stop at the fifth grade in Christian school?"

One vital lesson life has been taught to me: Don't argue with your wife. And, in this case, there was no good reason to argue with her. I smiled at her and said, "I agree; let's do middle school."

We rented another building and started a middle school and, a couple of years later, a high school as well. Before long, we knew that even the two buildings we had were too small. We didn't have enough space for all the students.

We began to pray for a place where we could build our own school. It took a couple years, but finally we found land and made a blueprint for the new school building. We needed funding, so we made a presentation to Compassion Christian Church of Savannah, Georgia.

Micky, the chairperson of their missions committee and a small man with a huge heart, asked, "Would this building be big enough for what you would like to do?" I explained that it would house our two hundred current students and allow us to add another fifty. He pressed in with his southern accent, "Why not build a second floor so you can add more students?" I told him we didn't have enough money for a second floor. He stared at me for a second, then asked, "Is this a matter of mind or a matter of faith?" I wasn't sure how to answer. "I'll say . . . both." We didn't have the money to pour the ground floor, and he was talking about adding a second floor. It sounded crazy. He challenged me, "Don't you think God can do it?" I knew the right answer and said it, even if I was doubtful, "I believe God can do it." He smiled, "Build the second floor."

Compassion Christian Church helped with a substantial donation, and we added a second floor to the blueprints.

We couldn't raise quite enough money, so we took out a loan from a US bank. Our payment was $15,000 a month, which was a lot for us. We thought we'd be paying it for ten to fifteen years, but God is good, and a couple of business leaders from Louisville stepped up and paid off our debt. About four years after taking out the loan, we were debt-free on the school.

I am so glad we added that second floor. Our two-story school grew to four hundred and then five hundred students. In fact, as I write this book, we are adding an extension so we can have more classrooms for our high school.

Message And Methods

Despite having a school, I would tell you that we are not educators. We are evangelizers. We exist to share Jesus, not to educate children. So, why do we educate children? Because it provides an opportunity for us to share Jesus with those students. We teach the Word of God at our school. The Bible is our main textbook. We have mandatory chapel every Wednesday. We pray at the beginning of the school day and before lunch. Some parents have shared with me that their child taught them how to pray. We've seen many students get baptized.

The school also allows us to strengthen the faith of Christian students so they can share Jesus with people outside the school.

Many of our students have become serious about walking with the Lord. They now lead worship in our weekly Bible hour and participate in our church on Sundays.

There's a saying, "The methods change. The message never does." That's what we have experienced with Proem. If you could go back to the beginning, you would see us proclaiming the same message we do today: Jesus is the sinless Son of God who came to earth to die for our sins and establish God's kingdom. When we put our faith in him and what he did on the cross and commit to following him, our sins are forgiven, and we have the hope of heaven. Until then, we join Jesus in his mission of seeking and saving the lost.

That is the message, and the message never changes.

The methods do.

What methods should we use to share Jesus and live out our mission? Whatever God presents to us. Whichever we can be effective in.

Camp ministry has been fruitful for us, as has sports ministry. Such ministries might not be effective for others. In our country, teaching English as a second language presents opportunities to tell people about Jesus. For a while, so did publishing a sports magazine.

We didn't expect to start a school—because we are evangelizers, not educators—but did it when we realized it would help affect our community for Jesus.

We've discovered that our school's impact goes even beyond the students who attend and their parents. A few years ago, Anna graduated from college with a degree in education. She and her husband Michael had been running his car repair shop. We were looking for a teacher and hired Anna. She was amazing with the kids in our school. Anna had not been a believer, but being a part of the school and the people she worked with led her to faith.

I love how, in 1 Corinthians 16:9, the Apostle Paul writes, "a great door for effective work has opened to me." That's what we are looking for—God opening great doors for effective work.

It makes me wonder: What will Proem be doing in thirty years? I don't know, but my guess is that it will surprise me. I do know the message won't change, and I do expect our methods will.

chapter nine

HOW CAN WE HELP?

J esus is traveling when he nears a town called Nain. "As he approached the town gate, a dead person was being carried out—the only son of his mother, and she was a widow" (Luke 7:12).

Jesus sees a mother who has just lost her only son. You wonder if it made Jesus think forward to when his widowed mother would watch her dead son being carried away from a cross. I don't know, but I do know that as followers of Jesus, we always enter into the pain of people who are hurting. "When the Lord saw her, his heart went out to her, and he said, 'Don't cry'" (Luke 7:13).

When we encounter a hurting person, our hearts may go out to the person. We might "mourn with those who mourn" (Romans 12:15), but Jesus always goes a step further. "Then he went up and touched the bier they were carrying him on, and the bearers stood still. He said, 'Young man, I say to you, get up!' The dead man sat up and began to talk, and Jesus gave him back to his mother" (Luke 7:14–15).

Kyle Idleman, senior pastor of Southeast Christian Church, says that with Jesus, there is "always an 'and.'" He never just felt compassion. He felt compassion and did something for the hurting person. As followers of Jesus, there should always be an "and." We hurt with the person, *and* we take action to relieve their pain.

We've tried to do that at Proem, and it's led to what we call our Helps Ministry.

We Help

Jesus saw a grieving mother. In Poland, we see problems all around us.

There are many broken marriages, often caused by alcohol addiction. Drinking is very much a part of our culture, and so many, especially men, drink to excess. Our attitude is that we will do everything we can to help. We invite people who want to be equipped not to continue falling into their same problems to come to us. We tell them that we will support them and be a family to them while they get sober.

There is also an abundance of struggling single mothers. We've seen this, especially in Łódź. It's heartbreaking. The single moms are often teenagers with no dad in the picture and no family willing to support them. Our stance is always, "We don't judge. We help." For instance, when we do Kontakt in Łódź we renovate shelters for single moms. We developed a relationship with the woman in charge of one shelter, who then came to our church with her husband, where both were saved.

We also have encountered many teenagers battling depression. They are struggling, and we listen, graciously share God's truth, and provide a place for them.

Increasingly, homeless people are looking to us for help. We provide shelter, food, and, always, the Word of God. They may need help for just a few days or perhaps several months to get back on their feet. No matter, we love them and want them to see their hope. We show them that not only are they welcome, but they are needed and can make a difference in our community.

We always remember that God gave us unconditional love, so it's not optional that we give it to others. And we know when we love hurting people, not only does the love we have to give come from God, but in a very real sense, we are also loving God. Jesus said, "Whatever you did for one of the least of these brothers and sisters of mine, you did for me" (see Matthew 25:40).

Our Counseling Ministry

With all the hurting people we encounter, we have always seen the need to provide counseling. For a long time, we just didn't have the right people to offer it in a significant way.

At one point, a family showed up at our TOMY church. The wife was a counselor, so with her, we started offering a few hours of professional counseling to the community each week.

Our counseling ministry really took off when Adam Pańczak, one of our pastors, and Agnieszka Piekarski went back to school for five years to get their degrees and certificates in counseling. Adam and Agnieszka are more than just trained; they have the compassion of Jesus, know how to build relationships, and are great leaders. Finally, we were able to offer full-time counseling, and when we did, the ministry took off. We now have two counselors working full-time and three part-time. They are all so busy that appointments with them need to be booked two weeks in advance. And it's not just people from our church. People from the community are coming for counseling as well. In fact, we recently learned that government officials at city hall are referring people to our counselors. Yes, Polish Roman Catholic city officials are referring people to a Protestant evangelical counseling center!

Counseling was happening at the TOMY church, but as it grew it required more space. At the same time, we were starting an after-school program. There was a lot of traffic in and out of the building, and it felt like we were bursting at the seams.

That's when we moved the counseling ministry out of the TOMY church and made the first floor of our new hotel in Tomaszów Mazowiecki a counseling center. We also renovated the ground floor, creating four counseling offices with their own separate entrances. It's a nice environment that allows us to better serve people.

We now have a few hours of counseling available in Łódź as well.

Over the years, we have sent dozens of people to rehab centers. We realize that's another need, and you know we love to meet needs, so we are currently asking God if perhaps we should start a rehab center in the near future.

More Help

When we talk about "Helps," it's a threefold ministry. One part of the ministry is helping people through counseling. The second is mission endeavors, both to and from other countries. I'll share more about that later. The third is providing help from TOMY church and from the camp in Zakościele in areas related to technology, equipment, and media.

It's fun to think about what the future may hold when it comes to technology and media.

People have suggested that we have the equipment, expertise, and connections to start our own movie production company. As I mentioned, Łódź is called "Hollylódź" because it's where the movie industry is located in Poland. A Christian movie production company based there would give Poles something other than secular movies to watch. We had thought of the movie production idea even before it was suggested to us. In fact, before our media department grew to its current size, our lighting technician Tomek Gużda graduated from the movie production academy in Łódź and made a few films, including one about people who smuggle Bibles into other countries.

We also look forward to using social media on a bigger scale. We now have two video update series: "As It Happens" and "Pray for Ukraine," on the Proem YouTube channel. We realize there are many opportunities for using social media that we have not yet explored.

We know that what we can do through our Helps Ministry is limitless. There will always be people in need, and as God continues to give us the resources, we'll find new ways to meet them.

Some needs are predictable, like helping people assimilate into society after dealing with addiction or helping single mothers land on their feet. Others are not, like the war in Ukraine that surprised everyone. We try to be ready to help wherever we can.

That's always been our attitude with Proem in Poland, but I never imagined God would lead Proem out of Poland.

chapter ten

To The Ends Of
The Earth

They were like creatures from another planet. They were missionaries, but aliens may not have been more foreign to me.

I was seven years old when two missionaries came to our small church. It made such a mark that I still remember their names: Gene Dulin and John Huk. They were from a faraway land called America and, using a translator, talked to us about sharing Christ in foreign countries.

When I grew up, there was no TV in Poland. The closest I came to leaving our country was reading books about the Wild, Wild West. These men were from the same country as the cowboys. They were from entirely different cultures, and they explained how we could share Jesus with people from entirely different cultures.

The thought was too much for me. *Really? Is it possible to go? Where would someone from a small Communist country like Poland go? Could I share Jesus with people who lived in faraway places?*

Shaking Things Up

Despite the confusion I experienced at seven years old, the Bible is very clear that we are to go. We are to go to our neighbors, our nation, and the ends of the earth to share the Good News of Jesus Christ.

For years, Poland in general and Proem specifically have been a destination for mission trips, especially for people from America.

When we were a Communist country, we could not openly share the Gospel. We couldn't even print Bibles. People could try to sneak Jesus into our country, but we weren't bringing him out of our country.

When we achieved freedom in the early 1990s, it was a struggle to establish churches, ministries, and outreach. We needed support from partners outside of Poland.

We became so used to others bringing the Gospel to us and mission trips coming to us that there was not much thought given to the idea of us going to other countries with the Gospel.

Then Brian Wright shook things up.

Brian is straightforward, quick to smile, and sarcastic and thoughtful. I first met him when he was the sports pastor at Southeast Christian Church in Louisville. He later became the missions pastor and was a vital part of our connection to Southeast for years. He left Louisville in 2004 to become the lead pastor of Foundry Church just outside of Kansas City, Missouri.

One day, Brian called and invited us to go on a mission trip. A group of about twelve from his church was going to Kenya to work with the poorest of the poor.

It was a novel idea. After years of receiving missionary teams, what would it look like for us to send a team? We knew Jesus's command to be his witnesses to the end of the earth, but we had never pictured us going.

We said yes.

It was time for us to go as Jesus commanded us and to share him with people outside of Poland.

Nine of us from Proem joined Brian's team in Kenya. It was amazing.

When we got home, we wondered, "Why don't we do more? Could we join other churches in serving places outside of Poland?"

One of our first opportunities emerged from that initial trip to Kenya. We had met Pastor Simon from Nairobi, who was hoping to construct a building to host ministry conferences. A couple of years later, a group of men from our church went and helped Simon with the construction.

As we continued to pray about where else God might want us to go, a group from Belarus came to our *Journey to Bethlehem* production in Zakościele. They loved what we were doing and said they wanted to do something similar. We told them we would help and organized a trip where a team went to Belarus to coach and assist them in doing their own version.

Compassion Christian Church does a "Refresh Retreat" at our camp for missionaries they support from around the world—Africa, Italy, and Ukraine. We reconnected with those missionaries at the retreats and began offering to send teams to help them with their ministry. That led to a series of trips to Zimbabwe.

The Holy Land And A Holy Gathering

I've been blessed to go on several trips to Israel. My third time there, I was praying in the Garden of Gethsemane. I told God, "Lord, this is a beautiful country, but I'm not coming to this country anymore unless I have something to do."

Immediately, I felt attacked by accusing thoughts, "Who are you to think you can do anything for Israel? What could you possibly offer?"

I am not a dynamic preacher or a musician. I tried to think of what I did best. Camps came to mind, which gave me a sense of peace.

When I got back to Poland the thought hit me again. I wondered about the kids in Israel. *How are they doing? What are their struggles?*

I assumed they had the same issues as kids in Poland. In one sense, that's true, but when you turn eighteen in Israel, both males and females go into the military. I talked to a friend in Israel who told me it was a time of intense pressure and tension for Israeli teenagers.

I asked what they do after their military service to refresh and was told that many who have the money will go on a trip to Thailand or Hong Kong, often for two or three months. They come back to Israel in even worse condition because they spend their time away on drugs, alcohol, and sex.

I thought we needed to reach them before they joined the military. If we could reach them with the message of Jesus, we might be able to protect them.

I asked some friends in Israel about whether it would be possible to put on cultural camps for Jewish teenagers.

I talked to a man in the parliament about us coming to do a camp for their teens. He was not enthusiastic until I told him we could find sponsors in America who would cover part of the cost. "Oh," his demeanor instantly changed, "how many students would you want to come?"

I was surprised. "Maybe twenty or thirty. Possibly fifty?"

He asked, "How about a thousand?"

Um, a thousand?

I shared the vision with churches in America for the next seven years. Then Charlie Vittitow, one of the mission's pastors from Southeast, asked, "Maui, are you still praying about the camp for Israeli teens? Southeast is ready to help." Our prayers had been answered.

In the summer of 2017, six people from Southeast, six from Proem, and 150 Israeli teenagers gathered for a week of camp in Jerusalem.

A couple of weeks earlier, I was in Washington, DC, at a conference on persecuted churches organized by the Billy Graham

Evangelistic Association. There were about eight hundred at the conference, and I was sitting at a table of ten people.

Each of us shared who we were and where we were from. Two men said they were Palestinian Christians from Jerusalem. I told them I was going to be there in two weeks. One of them asked why, and I explained that we were doing a camp for Jewish teenagers. He looked deep into my eyes and asked, "Why not for Palestinians?"

I said a quick prayer, asking the Holy Spirit to give me a good answer. I opened my mouth and said, "I guess because we don't have any connections with Palestinian Christians in Israel."

He gave me a big smile, "Now you do. My name is Mazen. You can come and visit us. We'd love to talk to you."

A few weeks later, I visited him at his Arabic-speaking church of about ninety Palestinian Christians in Old Town, within the city walls of Jerusalem. We prayed together, preached together, and then met with his leadership.

Mazen told me, "Maui, you won't believe it, but our dream is to take our young people to a camp somewhere. They don't even know how to ride a bike because everything is so dense here."

I said, "Mazen, I cannot promise anything, but God can do miracles."

Knowing Compassion Christian Church was connected to Palestinian Christians in Israel, I started talking to them. The next year, Compassion stepped up. We had about eight people from

Compassion, a few from Proem, and 150 Palestinian teenagers from the Bethlehem area at a youth camp.

The following year, we did two weeks of camp, one for Jewish kids and another in a different place for Palestinian kids.

I started to dream about doing a camp that would bring Jewish and Palestinian teenagers together. We sat down with leaders from both sides of the Holy Land, from Poland and from Southeast, to talk about the possibility.

I was so naïve.

There is such long-term, deeply rooted animosity—hatred, really—between Jews and Palestinians. I was told that the teenagers' parents on either side would never allow their children to be at a camp comprised of Palestinians and Jews together.

I didn't give up.

I told them, "I understand, but can't we overcome? What if you come to our camp in Poland? We could host five or six different nations for a cross-cultural camp. We could have thirty Jewish kids, thirty Palestinians, thirty Romani people, thirty Americans, and thirty Polish kids. They'll learn each other's languages and cultures."

To my surprise, they seemed to like the idea. We brought everyone to Poland to discuss the possibility, and . . . they agreed.

The next year, 2019, we had thirty young people from five people groups come. Monday was in Hebrew, Tuesday was in Romani, Wednesday was in Arabic, Thursday was in English, and

Friday was in Polish. We translated everything each day into the other languages.

We made each day a "cultural day." On Monday the Jewish people shared something from their culture. On Tuesday, people from Romania dressed in colorful robes and sang and danced until two in the morning.

One night we preached the Gospel and offered an invitation to accept Jesus as Lord and Savior. A few people from each group came forward and prayed to receive Christ.

The next day, a young Jewish man told me, "For the first time in my life, I talked to a Palestinian." A couple of hours later, a Palestinian said, "Maui, for the first time ever, I talked to a Jew!"

It was like honey to my ears.

On Friday some of the teenagers were baptized in the river that runs through our camp. It was an amazing experience. There were cheers and tears of joy and hugs given, regardless of what nation people were from.

After the baptisms we took all the kids on a field trip to Łódź. We had several buses ready. Before we left some of the Palestinian and Jewish leaders came to me, "Maui, could our groups be in one bus together? We'd like to connect and spend time together."

Wow.

The Ends

We are loving sending people on mission trips for so many reasons.

The people who go on these trips must raise their own funds. In fact, we ask everyone, even if they can afford to write their own check for their trip, to raise funds. It allows them to experience what others have been doing for years to support Proem. It also gives them an opportunity to share the trip and why they're doing it with people they ask for support, which may include people who don't know Jesus. Michael, the car mechanic in Tomaszów Mazowiecki, whose wife Anna is a teacher at our school, has gone on every trip to Zimbabwe. He got saved through Anna's testimony. He didn't have extra money for his first mission trip, but he had some extra car wheels. He's raised money by selling wheels for cars, letting everyone know what the fund will go toward. The local TV news even did a story about him including a beautiful interview about what we were doing in Africa.

Going on a trip is also beneficial because it teaches the participants to be flexible, available, and comfortable outside their comfort zone. You learn so much about yourself and working with others. On a mission trip, you experience the truth of Proverbs 27:17, "As iron sharpens iron, so one person sharpens another."

When you go somewhere, especially to a place where people are living in poverty, you better appreciate what you have. You may have complained about your rusty car in the past, but when you see people living without electricity or a woman carrying jars of water on her shoulders for five kilometers, you realize how blessed you are.

One last benefit of doing mission trips is that we have people who are not already part of Proem going on our trips. They might be parents of children in our school who don't know Jesus but are excited to join us in going to serve the needy in a foreign country. It allows us to witness to them in a different way.

Jesus taught, and it may be easiest to learn on a mission trip, that life really starts when you start living for people other than yourself.

Sitting as a seven-year-old, listening to two missionaries from a faraway land talk of going to other countries to share Jesus, I never would have believed that one day I would be one of those people or that I would lead people on such trips. And I can say it is: only God.

Only God.

chapter eleven

JUST SAY YES

G od's timing is always perfect.

Sometimes, his perfect timing is "Not yet." I think of the Israelites crying out to God for years to free them when they were in slavery in Egypt. And of Mary and Martha waiting for Jesus when their brother Lazarus was sick. And of our ten-year wait to find the land for our camp.

Sometimes, God's perfect timing is "right now." I think of God parting the Red Sea as the Egyptian army bore down on the Israelites, of God shutting the mouths of the lions when Daniel was thrown into their pit, and of the phone call we received in the Dominican Republic.

It was late February 2022, and ten of our male leaders traveled to the Dominican Republic to attend a conference organized by GO Ministries. GO is led by my long-time friend, Brook Brotzman. He and I started our ministries at the same time, and he had visited us in Poland. We were excited to go see his ministry in action and learn from what they were doing.

We arrived on Wednesday.

On Thursday, Russia attacked Ukraine. Some call it a war, but that implies two countries are at odds, and so engage in battle. This was not that. Russia, simply and without provocation, attacked its neighbor.

We received the news in the Dominican Republic. I will never forget seeing Sebastian Wójcik crying at his computer. He was on a video call with his wife, Monika. Sebastian served in the Polish military for several years before joining our staff, and when the war broke out, his wife immediately got a phone call saying he had forty-eight hours to report to the nearest military base. Sebastian was now serving in ministry. He and Monika have two small children. Their future was suddenly very uncertain.

Although we had just arrived in the Dominican Republic, we knew we all had to go back to Poland immediately.

From The Border To Camp

We left the next day, and when we arrived back home, we got a better idea of what was happening. Russia was mercilessly attacking the Ukraine. Bombs were landing in and destroying residential neighborhoods. Entire families were killed. Businesses were destroyed.

In most cases, Ukrainian men joined the military to help protect their country, and women and children had just a couple of hours to pack whatever they could fit into their cars and try to get out of the country. Sometimes, they couldn't take anything because their property was already destroyed. Most of these fleeing Ukrainians were coming across the border into Poland.

People were calling from the Ukraine and asking if they could come to our camp in Zakościele. Of course, we said yes. In fact, when we arrived back from the Dominican Republic on Saturday morning, there were already people from the Ukraine there.

Many of the Ukrainians didn't have cars and were using public transportation to get to the Poland/Ukraine border. Those trips could take up to twenty hours, and when they arrived, they were greeted with a ten to fifteen-hour line to wait in the frigid February cold to cross the border.

We started taking vans and buses so we could pick up people who were finally able to cross the border and take them to our camp at Zakościele.

Others arrived at our camp in their own cars. One time, eleven people slowly walked up to the camp. We began to explain where they could park their cars, but they said, "We all came in one car." They had packed eleven people into one car!

We made constant, repeated trips to the border. We quickly purchased a few more vans so we could transport more people. We also purchased some vans and trucks and donated them to Ukraine so they could be used inside the country to help people escape from the areas of intense fighting to the safer part of Ukraine in the west. A father of one of our former students, who had just graduated from our high school, called us and said, "We would like to donate an ambulance to Ukraine." We were shocked and asked him how he had an ambulance to donate. He paused and asked,

"Can you help me buy an ambulance in Poland so I can donate it?" We said, "Yes!" and soon he purchased a used ambulance that we sent to the Ukrainian military in a heated war zone.

A young man on our staff named Bogdan Linnik is a native Ukrainian who is married to a Polish woman and has been working with us for about five years, helping with media and technology. Bogdan is a tall, skinny young man with a beautiful, artistic soul. When the war broke out, he was living in Poland, but his family was still in Ukraine.

When I saw him on Sunday after we returned from the Dominican Republic, I told him, "Bogdan, you look tired." "I am," he sighed. "I've been driving to the border to bring my friends, my family, and people from my home to Zakościele." He was exhausted and it seemed clear he had rested barely a few hours in the past three days. I asked how many times he had been to the border since the war broke out. He said, "Just four." Knowing it's a five-hour drive each way and that sometimes you have to wait hours there before you can return, I asked if he had slept at all. He tried to smile, "I took a nap while I waited at the border."

I explained that driving that far without sleep could be life-threatening and asked him not to go again until he got some rest. He looked in my eyes and said, "Maui, how can I not go? My friends and family are there. There are people in need there. They're standing for ten hours in line to cross the border. What is it for me to spend five hours driving there?"

I was almost in tears. I told him I would approve of one more trip if he promised to get some sleep after it. He said, "I promise."

Bogdan is a great servant of the Lord, and he remains the point person in Proem's relationship with Ukraine.

At The Camp Refugee Center

With all that was happening in Ukraine and all the Ukrainians now in Poland, we knew we needed more, a *lot* more. We needed more food, clothing, medicine, everything! Our guys created a webpage within twelve hours. Through that site, people could find out what was needed and make donations. People were so generous. There was often a line of cars coming to Zakościele bringing much-needed supplies.

Our storage rooms filled up quickly, and we soon turned our big tent into a warehouse for clothing.

We ended up receiving so many donations that we were able to send hundreds of trucks of various sizes (even semis) full of supplies to the shelters in Ukraine to help those who were not trying to cross the border. We eventually sent *hundreds of tons* of goods to Ukraine.

The capacity at our camp is two hundred people, and we had two hundred beds available. But with Ukrainian refugees flooding our camp, we kept adding more beds and soon turned our dining hall into an emergency dormitory. Our kitchen staff figured out new places for people to eat and cooked continuously to feed them. Starting on February 24, they provided hundreds of Ukrainians with three meals a day, seven days a week, for over three months.

We also gave out soap, shampoo, toothbrushes, toothpaste, and other items. We knew we had to say yes and find a way to provide whatever people needed.

The biggest need was emotional, as we were serving people who had just experienced traumatic wartime events. They were separated from their families, sometimes not knowing who was or wasn't alive back home and having no idea how long it all might continue.

The further east you go in Europe, the more the man plays a bigger role in a family. We sat with women and their children and, knowing the war could continue for some time and their new reality might last indefinitely, asked them, "Where do you want to go to settle down until the war is over? Germany? Holland? Switzerland? Somewhere else in Poland?" Most looked at us, confused, and answered, "How can I decide? My husband is fighting in the war, and I cannot call him."

We gave everyone opportunities to open their hearts and share the devastation they were feeling. We would listen for hours but could not rest because there were still more people to listen to and more needs to meet. All we could do was lean on God and trust him to supply us with what we needed.

I remember one day when a man came into our office, sat down, and started weeping. I asked what was wrong. He explained, "I just learned that my brother was killed in the war." Sometimes it feels like there are no words you can say.

We told the Ukrainians we were Christians and looked to God for our help. We invited everyone to a daily prayer time at seven in the evening, at which we would pray for everyone individually and collectively, pray for their families back home, and pray for peace in Ukraine.

The government required us to report the names of each person who came in from Ukraine and to have their passports reviewed. I suppose you never know who might try to cross the border with evil intentions, but we never had anyone come through with ulterior motives. Every single person was escaping the turmoil in Ukraine. We look at that as God's providence. We were doing his work in that situation, and he protected us from anyone who might try to bring us harm.

We submitted our list of the new people who had arrived each day. In three months, we had about one thousand Ukrainians come to our camp.

In fact, without our asking, Google Maps changed the name of our camp from the Proem Christian Center to the Proem Refugee Center. Isn't that amazing? People who had no connection to us recognized what was being done, that we were providing a place where refugees could come and survive.

It wasn't easy to turn our camp into a refugee center, especially in God's "right now" timing, but we were honored to do it, and we had no choice. We said yes because we are God's children and want to be like him. We read in Deuteronomy 10:18–19, "He defends the cause of the fatherless and the widow, and loves the foreigner residing among you, giving them food and clothing. And you are to love those who are foreigners."

Camp Is Coming

As the refugees started flooding into our camp in the last days of February, we realized we had to cancel everything we had planned for March and April. Although some people may have been disappointed, everyone understood and supported our decision.

We usually begin registration for our summer camps on March 1 and sell out all the spaces within a couple of hours. We postponed registrations because of the turmoil that was happening, but a couple of weeks later, we thought it was time to open them up. We hoped the war might be over by summer, and if we were going to be back on our regular schedule come summer, we needed the campers to register.

The war was not over in the next month or two. Time passed, and we began to ask all the "What if?" questions, like, "What if summer camp season starts and we still have Ukrainians living at the camp?" It was a desperate feeling, and we knew we had to find an alternative.

Someone let us know that there had been an advertisement in the Tomaszów Mazowiecki newspaper in February for a hotel that was for sale. We contacted the owner to see if it was still available and if he might allow us to rent it. We figured we could relocate the people from Zakościele to the hotel and still be able to host camps.

The owner said no. It was not for rent. We persisted, but he was adamant that renting was out of the question. As a businessman, he could not afford to take the risk of what transient, unscreened refugees might do to his property.

We didn't know what to do, so we...made a video.

Tomek Gużda and I went to the other side of the street from the hotel, and Tomek recorded one of our "As It Happens" videos. I shared that perhaps God wanted us to have this place as we urgently needed to relocate the Ukrainians who were still at our camp.

Some responded by asking what we would do with a fully functional hotel with forty-five rooms once the war ended. I was glad they asked. I told them we had wished for a facility like this for years. Three years earlier, during the war in Afghanistan, Afghani people escaped to Poland, and we would have had a place to house them. They asked to stay in our camp, but it wasn't possible at the time because it was summer and it was filled with teenagers. Five years prior, we could have helped people who were escaping Africa by crossing the Mediterranean in makeshift boats and who drowned by the hundreds.

I also explained that we had been working with families in Tomaszów Mazowiecki with our new counseling ministry and had been hoping to have a place for teenagers who were suffering from depression or as a shelter for single moms or abused wives. The hotel could also be used for people coming out of addiction rehab.

We were still in a dire situation, so we . . . made another video.

I shared that we know God works miracles and were praying he would provide the funds to purchase the hotel.

He did.

People started giving substantial donations. To give you a comparison, it took us ten years to raise the money for the down payment for our camp. When we bought our school, we had to get a loan from an American bank. But to buy a fully functioning hotel with a kitchen, restaurant, and forty-five rooms, it took us just *eight weeks* to raise all the funds.

We called the owner to inquire, "Are you still selling the hotel?" He asked, "Why do you have the money?" And we said, "Yes!"

We signed the contract on the last day of May. The owner handed us the keys to the hotel, which was fully equipped with dishes and silverware, and with sheets for all the beds.

I spoke with the Ukrainians that evening and told them a miracle had happened. The next day, they would be like the Israelites leaving Egypt and heading toward the Promised Land. (Ironic since we had considered the camp our Promised Land.)

On June 1, the remaining refugees in Zakościele ate breakfast at the camp and lunch in the hotel.

We were happy for them and relieved for us. After having two hundred or more people at the camp for three months, we knew there was a lot of work to do to prepare for the first week of camp, which was only a couple of weeks away.

But the day before we signed the contract on the hotel, we got a phone call from a Ukrainian orphanage in Zytomir. They said, "We'd like to bring our children to your camp for one or two weeks. Could we do that?"

And we said . . . yes.

So, on June 1, we transported the Ukrainians to the care of our hotel staff and immediately returned to Zakościele just as two buses pulled in filled with traumatized Ukrainian children. We spent the next two weeks doing camp for the orphans. At the same time, we did everything we could to prep for our summer programming, and then, as the orphans left, the Polish campers started showing up.

The Answer Is Yes

In Matthew 25, Jesus speaks of the day when he will sit on his glorious throne and will separate people "as a shepherd separates the sheep from the goats" (Matthew 25:32).

Jesus will welcome the righteous sheep into his kingdom, saying,

> "'For I was hungry and you gave me something to eat, I was thirsty and you gave me something to drink, I was a stranger and you invited me in, I needed clothes and you clothed me, I was sick and you looked after me, I was in prison and you came to visit me.'" (Matthew 25:35–36)

Jesus explains that the righteous will be confused, asking,

> "'Lord, when did we see you hungry and feed you, or thirsty and give you something to drink? When did we see you a stranger and invite you in, or needing clothes and clothe you? When did we see you sick or in prison and go to visit you?'"

> "The King will reply, 'Truly I tell you, whatever you did for one of the least of these brothers and sisters of mine, you did for me.'" (Matthew 35:37–40)

They said yes. They said yes to people in need, perhaps not even realizing that in doing so, they were saying yes to Jesus.

Jesus then turns to those on the left and tells them to depart from him. Why?

They didn't say yes.

> "Then he will say to those on his left, 'Depart from me, you who are cursed, into the eternal fire prepared for the devil and his angels. For I was hungry and you gave me nothing to eat, I was thirsty and you gave me nothing to drink, I was a stranger and you did not invite me in, I needed clothes and you did not clothe me, I was sick and in prison and you did not look after me.'

> "They also will answer, 'Lord, when did we see you hungry or thirsty or a stranger or needing clothes or sick or in prison, and did not help you?'

> "He will reply, 'Truly I tell you, whatever you did not do for one of the least of these, you did not do for me.' (Matthew 25:41–45)

The difference was whether or not they said yes.

We know that a person going to heaven or not is all about whether they say yes to Jesus as their Savior and Lord. But when you say yes to who Jesus is and what he did for you, you then say yes to what Jesus asks and what he wants you to do for others. As Jesus's half-brother James tells us:

> Do not merely listen to the word, and so deceive yourselves. Do what it says . . . . Religion that God our Father accepts as pure and faultless is this: to look after orphans and widows in their distress and to keep oneself from being polluted by the world. (James 1:22, 27)

We've been asked about our motivation for doing what we did. People point out that it disrupted the successful ministry we were doing and created a tireless, seemingly endless ministry for us. Why did we do it?

Because we follow Jesus. Jesus tells us the greatest commandments are to love God and love your neighbor. The Ukrainians are our neighbors. How could we not jump in and do everything we could to love them?

In a situation like that, you don't need to think or pray about your answer, you don't sit down and evaluate the circumstances or make plans; you just say yes.

You say yes when there is a need and step into that gap with action.

You say yes to the hungry, yes to the thirsty, yes to the stranger, and yes to the prisoner.

You say yes to the least of these: yes to the widow, yes to the orphan.

You say yes to carrying the burdens of someone who cannot carry their own.

You say yes to touching the sick.

You say yes to the unknown.

You say yes to the sleepless nights.

You say yes, no matter how long your yes may be.

Did saying yes force us to change all our plans? Yes, it did. But as the Apostle Paul put so well:

> Was I fickle when I intended to do this? Or do I make my plans in a worldly manner so that in the same breath I say both "Yes, yes" and "No, no"?

> But as surely as God is faithful, our message to you is not "Yes" and "No." For the Son of God, Jesus Christ, who was preached among you by us—by me and Silas and Timothy—was not "Yes" and "No," but in him it has always been "Yes." For no matter how many promises God has made, they are "Yes" in Christ. And so through him the "Amen" is spoken by us to the glory of God. (2 Corinthians 1:17–20).

chapter twelve

RELATIONSHIPS FIRST

W̶hen you drive into the camp at Zakościele, you see this sign: "Relationships First."

We have three distinctives at Proem, three core values we always live by, and the first is "Relationships First."

Being a ministry in Poland, you may suspect the next is "Pierogis Second." It's not, but we do love pierogis.

I'll tell you the second and third later. First, I'd like to explore why we value relationships and how this core value has guided us and led to fruit in our ministry.

First

After declaring everything he had made good, God's first pronouncement about the first human was that it is not good for man to be alone. That man, Adam, already had a relationship with God, but something was still missing.

We were made not only for God but also for each other.

Regardless of our personalities, we are all relational people. We may express it in different ways, but it's vital for each of us. We all need to belong.

Relationships are a driving force in our ministry. We've found that with strong relationships and mutual understanding, we can be honest with each other, serve happily together, and develop what we call "partnership in the spirit of togetherness."

There is no fast track to developing relationships, but if you invest in them, the relationship itself will be the reward, and you will see results in due time.

I want to give you just a brief peek at how putting relationships first plays out with the people we are ministering to and the people who support our ministry.

People We Are Ministering With

Relationships are integral for the Proem staff.

It actually begins *before* you join our staff. We don't hire people just because they have a great resume and can give good answers in an interview. Whenever possible, we want people we already know, who are already, in some sense, one of us, to join our team. That way, we really know the person and the relationships are already established.

You see it in our staff. They like each other. They have fun together. They spend eleven months of the year working together and then . . . choose to go on vacation together. That may sound crazy to some, but they truly love each other. It's the result of relationship-first ministry.

People We Are Ministering To

In my long life, I've participated in many leadership seminars and read many leadership books. John Maxwell says everything rises and falls on leadership.

I believe that's true.

At the same time, if you don't have relationships with the people you are leading, you could learn the skills of leadership but end up practicing techniques rather than truly leading.

So, yes, leadership is vital. But relationships come first. Leadership, in the context of relationship, gives hope for growth and progress.

The same is true with vision. Proverbs 29:18 tells us, "Where there is no revelation, people cast off restraint." That's true, and I love vision, but I believe the vision should be for people and relationships.

Some leaders may have a vision for growth, but growth is made up of people. Other leaders have visions for big buildings, but what matters is the people inside them.

Still, other leaders are all about strategy. They love to predetermine their action steps. I believe in strategy, but I would say predetermining the correct action steps is impossible if you don't know the people to whom you're ministering. The best strategy is a response to their real needs.

Relationships first. It's in the DNA of Proem.

As you've read this book, you have seen countless examples of it.

We did camps to build relationships with the kids who attended.

We brought in chiropractors from America so we could create relationships with the people who came in for their appointments.

We organized basketball tournaments and joined city basketball leagues to build relationships with the other players.

We opened tea houses and coffee shops to serve as relationship incubators.

We teach English, parenting, and other classes. Why do we do that? Is the reason to meet people's needs? Yes! But also, we need to meet people we don't know so we can start relationships with them.

We start churches by moving into a city and getting to know the people who live there.

With the people we are ministering to, it's all about relationships.

People Who Support Our Ministry

Proem owes everything to the people and churches who have supported us over the years. Can you guess what we believe comes first with our supporters? Yes, it's relationships.

With any potential partner, we say, "Let's get to know each other first. We want you to come and see how we do things at Proem. And we'd love to send one of our team to spend time with you and see your ministry context." That way, we would get to know each other and see what we could do for each other.

I hope the other party is not looking at us and thinking, "What can Maui and Proem do for me?" and I don't want to be thinking that about them. We want to get to know each other, form a relationship, and then ask the Lord what he wants us to do together. We come up with common goals we can pursue together, which helps eliminate selfishness and create a win-win situation.

It's easy to think people from America don't need anything. America is a big country with a lot to offer and many different cultures. But one thing we offer is a chance for an American, who may not have the chance otherwise, to go to another country. As they journey to Poland, they will experience God and see him working in a different way. People on the mission trip will get out of their comfort zone and often use their gifts in new ways. This can be an incredible accelerator of spiritual growth. People may go home ready to step up in serving or leading.

Internships have become another mutually beneficial highlight of our partnership with churches. We couldn't function as effectively without interns. It's also been a help to the sending churches, and we've been able to send interns from Poland to our partner churches in America.

We don't give interns menial jobs but important responsibilities that prepare them to become the next generation of leaders. We give them a "practice field" to build relationships and do ministry.

The same is true with the interns we have sent to Southeast Christian Church, beginning with Rafal and Agnieszka. Another intern we sent—Magda—was invited by Pastor Bob Russell to come on stage in the big auditorium during a packed Sunday morning service. Bob introduced Maga, and she announced, "I'm with Proem ministries. Thank you for allowing me to share what we do."

Bob said, "It's good to have you here with us. We wish you a good time. Do you have something to share?"

"Bob," she asked, "do you know what you call a person who speaks three languages?"

Bob responded, "No, I don't."

Magda said, "They're trilingual."

Bob laughed, "That's nice."

She continued. "Bob, do you know what you call a person who speaks two languages?"

Bob answered, "I don't know what?"

She told him, "Bilingual," then, "Wait, that's not all. Bob, do you know what you call a person who speaks one language?"

Bob said, "No, I don't."

Magda smiled, "An American."

There were thousands of people in the auditorium, and Bob could not calm them down. They laughed for several minutes, and Bob loves telling the story to this day.

Our exchange program with Southeast continues today.

We would tell you that our partners in America have meant everything to us, and I believe they would tell you they have received a lot from our partnership as well.

It's all based on relationships. Casual observers are surprised when they see the scope of our ministry to learn that we only have about twelve partner churches. Part of the reason is that we want deep relationships, not just a church that will send an occasional check or team.

We would love to have more partners and pray we will. We have found it nearly impossible to introduce ourselves to an unknown church and get a response. (Remember the thousand unanswered letters I sent out in 1994?) We need more exposure to more churches in the States. If we do get more partners, you can be sure we'll put relationships first.

We also have some partners who are not churches.

A few businesspeople support us and make a real difference in our ministry. Some have connected us with others who might be interested in partnering with us, but it's never an easy process.

We also seek to partner with Christian colleges. When we do, Proem can become a destination for students interested in the type of ministries we are doing. We've had American college students come do summer internships, which also creates the possibility of staying long-term. That benefits us and the college. We hope to build more relationships with more colleges, in America and beyond. We have limited connections to these colleges, but the potential for our internship program is limitless.

Every partner we have is immensely valuable, and I don't want to offend any of them, but I feel led to mention a few.

Throughout the book, I've mentioned our two biggest supporters—in terms of financial support and involvement from their people—Southeast Christian Church in Louisville, Kentucky, and Compassion Christian Church in Savannah, Georgia.

Mount Pleasant Christian Church in Greenwood, Indiana, came years ago to help with a basketball camp and has been supporting us ever since. Their pastor, Chris Philbeck, blessed their team member Guy Quinnette to lead over thirty short-term trips to Poland.

Another key partner is Sunnybrook Christian Church in Stillwater, Oklahoma. Jim Johnson, their lead pastor, has visited us in Poland several times. Mac and Olivia Johnson, Jim's son and daughter-in-law, moved to Poland and are helping to lead our team in Piotrków.

Brian Wright has been a real catalyst for our ministry. Brian and I have spent lots of time dreaming together and asking, "Why not try?" He has become a dear friend. Brian is a great listener who I can bounce ideas off and know I'll get honest feedback.

I could fill a book bragging about the churches and individuals who have played an indispensable role in Proem's growth. If I tried to list them all, I know I'd leave someone out, so I won't try. But the truth is none of them help us receive praise, and they all know how much we love and appreciate them.

It's relationships first—with the people we minister with, the people we minister to, and the people who support our ministry.

Ultimately, it's not about our relationships with people but about our relationships with people leading people into a relationship with God.

It's relationships first and, in the end, it will be relationships last. Someday everyone who said yes to Jesus will gather in heaven, where we will experience relationships with each other and God like we never have before. We want everyone to be there. We know relationships will be last, so we put relationships first.

chapter thirteen

PROCESS OVER PROGRAM
PRODUCT

S ome leaders are task driven. Others are goal-, purpose-, or strategy-driven.

There's nothing wrong with any of that. In fact, I'm for all of it. But I believe if we focus on what we have to do or what we want to accomplish, we can sacrifice the process—*how* we do what we do, and possibly the people involved. And I believe the people and process are far more important.

People hear that and ask, "Maui, you don't care about the results?" I do, big time. We have a plan. We have goals in mind. But *how* we're going to accomplish them is more important.

You may have a goal and be able to reach that destination in either twelve or twenty-four months. If you reach your objective in twelve months but lose people along the way because you didn't value your relationships with them or because of how you did ministry, that's not good. I'd much rather take twice as long but with a process guided by love, integrity, and wisdom.

I've seen so many leaders who are too driven by their goals and submit everything to them. Too often those leaders lose something vital along the way—it might be relationships, or their integrity, or their first love for Jesus. At Proem we have goals, but we say that goals are the product, and we always place the process over the product.

Instead of submitting ourselves to the goal, we submit ourselves to God. We trust that if we try to do ministry in a way that honors him, he will honor us by allowing us to achieve what he wants us to in his timing.

I tell our staff that instead of setting our plans and objectives and then praying for God to bless them, we will pray to God to show us what he is already blessing. That way, we are following his lead instead of trying to lead him.

I've wondered what led me to have this approach. Perhaps it was beginning ministry during Communism and then in Poland's shift to democracy. So much was uncertain. During Communism, we were never sure if the government would shut down our plans. At the birth of democracy, it was impossible to predict what life would be like or what might happen next. During those times, we had plans but couldn't fill in too much of the details. We had dreams, but we held them loosely. We just knew whatever happened, we wanted to share the Gospel with people and do it in a way that honored God.

That attitude has stayed with me and has become part of Proem's heartbeat. You see it in all kinds of ways.

Number Of Campers

We started our ministry with camps. For a while, camps were all we did. Whether or not our ministry was successful was based entirely on our camps, but even still, we never set a goal for the number of campers. Instead, we focused on the process. We wanted to do everything in a way that honored God and the people who were volunteering at the camp. We endeavored to make the camp worth the time of the campers and to make sure they left having experienced God and better knowing Jesus.

But how many campers should we serve? If we reach the number of kids God provides, that's a success.

The only numbers we ever focused on were about capacity. We want to have as much capacity at the camp as possible so that God can send all the teenagers he wants to us.

New Ministries With No Plans

As you've heard, after camps, we started planting churches, a school, and then a counseling ministry.

The impact of each has exceeded our expectations, in part because we didn't really have specific expectations.

We didn't start Proem with a master plan of camps, then churches, then schools, then counseling. Our plan was to share Jesus with people in Poland.

As we listened for God's whisper and followed his lead, he showed us the needs of our neighbors, and as we sought to meet them, new ministries happened.

Perhaps the best example of this is with our church plants.

Church Plants

We have sent people to cities around Poland. You may be surprised by what we don't tell them. We don't say, "We need you to plant a church within three years and have elders appointed and $100,000 in offerings within five years."

We say nothing like that.

We give no due dates and no number expectations.

I'm not saying it's wrong. Others may do it that way. That's fine for them. It's just not us.

We say, "Go to this city. Meet the people there. Develop relationships with them. Be with them and be a blessing to them. If the Lord is willing, we'll start a church there, or maybe a preschool, or perhaps a counseling ministry." You may be interested to know that our first church plant in Tomaszów Mazowiecki is now one of the ten largest evangelical churches in Poland.

What do we mean by "Lord willing?"

In the Bible, God didn't tell us how many churches he wanted us to start and within how many years. He told us he would bless us so we could be a blessing. That's what we do. He commissioned us to make disciples. That's what we do.

If a new church is birthed, that's great. If a church does not end up being the result, that is not a failure because we didn't go there to plant a church. If our people went and showed that city Jesus by being a blessing in his name, and if they shared Jesus, that's a success. What would a failure look like? Going but not building relationships or sharing Christ.

Relationships

I've talked throughout the book about our emphasis on relationships, but I will never tire of sharing why and how we put relationships first. Another way to think about it is in process versus product.

Let's say a church discovers there are hungry people in their area and decides to give out boxes of food. You can give out one hundred boxes of food or one thousand boxes of food. Which would be more successful?

The obvious answer is one thousand.

Except I don't think that's the *right* answer.

The best answer is relationships first. If you give boxes of food to one thousand people, but because there are so many and because logistics take so much time you cannot develop relationships with them, I would not call that success. If you can give out one hundred boxes and actually build relationships with the recipients, I think that would be far more successful. If the only way to develop a relationship is to limit your food distribution to one person, I would give food to one person. If you develop a relationship with one and bring that person to a saving knowledge of Christ, it may eventually influence a lot more than a thousand people.

Sure, big numbers are exciting. But:

• Elijah had times when he was faithful to God and felt like the only one.

- Jeremiah faithfully shared God's Word but never saw a single person repent.

- Jesus sometimes had huge crowds, but at the end, as he stood trial and was nailed to the cross, no one was left.

Someday we will stand before God and I hope to hear him say, "Well done, good and faithful servants." I don't think it will be about the numbers. I believe it will be about how we did ministry, how we loved God and people. Were we good? Were we faithful?

So, I'll choose process over product every time.

chapter fourteen

TEAM LEADERSHIP

From the beginning of Proem we have been blessed with amazing leaders.

I think of Exodus 17, when the Israelites were in battle, and their leader Moses was pleading with God for them with his arms up in prayer. The Israelites were successful only when Moses's arms were up and so, as he grew tired, Aaron and Hur held his hands up.

In the early years of Proem, I felt I had faithful leaders holding up my arms as I led. Now, I'm more often in the position of holding others up as they lead.

At the beginning of the ministry, it was my responsibility to do nearly everything. Of course, we had leaders to help with camp. We would have 150 students at camp and needed fifteen camp leaders. The camp leaders started out doing relatively small things, but many grew into essential leaders as we have increasingly moved to team leadership.

Adding Leaders

Every time someone asks me how we've found so many great leaders, I smile, and I think of Epaphras. No, Epaphras never worked for Proem. He is someone mentioned three times in the New Testament—twice in Colossians and once in Philemon. Paul holds him in high esteem, calling Epaphras his "dear fellow servant" and "a faithful minister of Christ." But what I especially took note of is that Paul called Epaphras "one of you."

That statement has been a focus of mine as we've built our team. We prioritize trusting leadership to someone who has already been "one of us."

It fits with our "relationships first" core value. We believe everything starts with relationships, and that is certainly true with people we bring on as leaders. Our approach is to look for people who have been with us, perhaps even grew up in our ministry, and then to see if they can also lead. In a sense, we don't hire people; we raise up people to positions of leadership. We do use assessments in considering potential new staff, but much more important to us is that we already know the person and what we know about them. We know that someone who is one of us already loves and has ownership in our ministry. We don't want someone who is paid to go to war; we want someone who goes to war because it's personal. You could say we want warriors, not mercenaries. People who are one of us have proven themselves and are more likely to go the extra mile when needed.

Not only are we seeking people with whom we first have a relationship, but we also prioritize people who put relationships first.

We've discovered that leadership, skills, and methods can be taught, but you can't really learn to love people and build relationships. That's much less about techniques and more about your heart. We want people on our team who have a heart for people.

I don't know if our way is best for everyone, but it is the best way for us. Some might be critical of our approach. I know there are some downsides. For instance, because we generally develop and hire "from within," we may not get as much of a different perspective and new ideas as if we hired "from without." However, we will take the upside of knowing the person and knowing that they fit into our ministry.

Raising Up Leaders

One of the most rewarding things in leading Proem has been seeing the children of our staff take leadership roles.

Most of our staff started as campers in their teens. They've been "one of us" for most of their lives. But their kids have literally been a part of our ministry since the day they were born.

There's a stereotype that the kids of people in ministry rebel and turn away from God. While I'm sure there's an example or two of that in Proem, it's been amazing how many of our leaders' kids are now becoming leaders in our ministry. They've had parents who were great examples and are now following in their footsteps.

Children of ministry leaders may turn away from the church and ministry because they see the ministry as a rival. They think, "Dad was so involved in ministry he didn't have time for me." We see very little of that, I believe, because we have involved kids in the ministry from the beginning. Proem ministry keeps families together rather than separating them.

We don't push our kids into anything but find they want to join us when they see our enthusiasm and the fun we're having. And we're not afraid to ask them to step up and participate.

I think of Boris, my grandson, who is twelve years old. He played the student of a rabbi in *Journey to Bethlehem*. That's fun for him, but it's also hard work. We do the program twenty to thirty times a day for three straight weekends. I believe that builds something vital in him at an early age.

Boris has gotten involved because of his parents. Our son grew up in our ministry and did everything with us. He met Agata, who would become his wife, as they both served with us in their teen years. Later, they got married and found employment outside of Proem, but eventually, both joined us full-time in our ministry.

The kids in our ministry get involved with easy first steps in our productions, camps, and ministries according to their gifts, passions, and capacity.

One great example is with our singers. For years we have had our amazing band, Exodus 15. Lately, we have been calling them Exodus Old because there is now an Exodus Young. Estera Pańczak is one of the original worship leaders at TOMY Church, and now her two daughters, Noemi and Miriam, are also singing. They're not the only kids of ministry leaders in the band. Agata Piekarski, Rafal's and Agnieszka's daughter, sings. So does Tomek Crozier. His brother David helps with the sound and media. Natalia

Wawrzyniak plays the violin, and her brother Nathan Wawrzyniak is learning to run sound.

Another benefit to having these young people involved in leading worship is that Tomek, Miriam, Noemi, and Agata are the same age as many of the kids at camp. Seeing someone your own age on stage makes it easier for the campers to relate and connect.

We even have the next group—Exodus Kids—coming along. They participate in appropriate places, like the camps for younger children and Christmas carol singing for *Journey to Bethlehem*. Michał and Karolina Kupczyk's two daughters and Basha, Przemek's and Agata's daughter (and my granddaughter) sing with Exodus Kids. They're not afraid to go on the stage to sing and dance. In fact, when Exodus 15 recorded their latest CD, some of the children did backup vocals, including my grandson Boris, who rapped.

Kids are not just involved in the music ministry. For instance, Tomek and Stephanie Gużda's son is sports-oriented, so when we do soccer or basketball camps, he is very involved in that as well. Their daughter, Sara, is singing with Exodus Kids.

When we build relationships with these kids, we find their strengths and encourage them to work in those areas, just like we do with adult leaders. Then, as they participate, we come alongside and support them.

It's such a blessing to have all these kids involved in ministry. At the same time, they are learning their talents, developing their skills and . . . perhaps being raised up to be staff members of Proem one day.

Connecting Future Leaders

We have a great new program geared toward the next generation of leaders called "the Connect Program."

The church is concerned because fewer and fewer people worldwide feel called to ministry. Churches are diminishing, and Bible colleges are struggling. There is a huge need for young people to be pointed at and prepared for ministry.

Connect is a two-year Christian leadership development program, with weekend-long sessions every other month. We invite up to thirty young adults who are at least eighteen years old to participate.

The program includes Friday, Saturday, and Sunday activities in Zakościele and Tomaszów Mazowiecki.

We spend the first evening at one of our homes with Rafal, Daniel, John, and other leaders. We have supper, talk to the participants openly, and encourage them to ask all their questions. We tell them some of Proem's history. The young people can't believe that not only did we start without computers, but there was even a time when we didn't even have a typewriter. They listen with their mouths wide open as they learn Zaba, who was the principal of their school, started in the ministry by washing windows. We also share our values, wanting these young people to see that the context and methods of ministry change, but the message is always the same.

The next day, we offer a class in which we discuss—from a Biblical context and including teaching from psychologists—the four areas of human life: the spirit, soul, body, and mind. These are college students, so we provide intense training.

On Sunday, all the Connect participants have the opportunity to get involved in the church in multiple ways. During the summer months, they can help us with camp.

As the program continues, we teach concepts from the Bible, our ministry, and about leadership. We also provide all kinds of hands-on training.

Our hope is to raise these young people up to be leaders. As Jesus did with his disciples, we want to share our lives with and show these young people practical ways to grow in and practice leadership. We hope some will become leaders in Proem but would also be thrilled if they end up serving in other ministries.

Our dream is to take all our students to the Holy Land for the last session of this two-year program to walk in Jesus's footsteps.

Developing Leaders

We believe it's our responsibility to develop the leaders God gives us, and that starts with the passion God has put in their hearts.

When someone shows interest in working with us, we don't say, "Great, because we have a need, and we're going to put you in that area." Instead, we ask, "What's your calling? What do you want to do?" If the ministry area they say fits our vision, we love putting them where they will love serving.

We often have someone start by taking a position for just one year. That way, especially if it is the rare person from outside

Proem, they will learn about us, and we'll learn about them. They're increasingly becoming one of us, and we can see their abilities and availability, as well as whether they are truly dedicated to the cause and will be a good fit. After the year, if we feel they are qualified and still want to be with us, we may ask them to join our team.

By positioning people in areas where they are gifted, you are setting them up to succeed. You are also building on strengths instead of the more difficult task of strengthening weaknesses.

Another benefit of hiring people who have become one of us and are a good fit and assigning them to an area of passion and strength is that it helps us retain leaders. If we, because we have a need, ask someone to serve in an area of weakness or where they lack passion, they will lack enthusiasm and be less likely to stick around. However, we have had very little turnover through the years because our leaders serve where they are most effective.

We also believe that leaders are learners. If we are going to continue to develop, we need to grow our knowledge and abilities. Many of our leaders are still students in online schools:

- Agnieszka Piekarski graduated from counseling school.

- Edyta Wawrzyniak got further training in finances.

- Zaba Crozier continued her education in administration.

- Agata Dwulat received more training in teaching ethics.

While we believe in continuing education, we find the best learning happens through experience, learning by doing. Everyone at Proem has heard, "Tell me, I'll forget. Show me, maybe I'll remember. Involve me; for sure, I will learn." Our simple strategy is to tell them, to show them, and, especially, to involve them. This is what Jesus did with his disciples. He taught them, but mostly, he walked with them, set an example, and gave them the opportunity to do what he was doing.

We give future leaders responsibilities in our ministry even before they officially become leaders. We also ask them to be involved in decision-making. We'll meet and pray together to talk through any major decisions. We seek their ideas and wisdom, believing they've earned the right to be heard.

Key Leaders

In Hebrews 11, God gives us a kind of hall of fame of leaders in the Bible, and I thought it would be appropriate to talk about some of Proem's key leaders.

Zaba Crozier

When we first started the ministry, Zaba had just graduated from computer college and was in my youth group. We purchased a little downtown office in the center of Warsaw and renovated it. I asked the youth group who would like to help clean up after the painting was done. She said, "I'll help. I've got a couple of weeks free as I wait for a job offer."

When we were done with the office, I asked if she had received an offer. She said no, so I asked if she would be willing to answer the phones and make coffee for people who were coming to talk about our ministry.

After a few months, she was still there and had learned to make good coffee. (I might have kept her around even if she didn't make good coffee, but that certainly helped.)

One day, the editor of the secular sports magazine I talked about earlier in the book came to our office. Zaba was so nervous she spilled coffee on the table and all over that man. We laugh about it to this day.

Serving in ministry may not have been what Zaba thought she'd spend her life doing, but God had different plans for her. She was our first hire and today is one of the primary leaders of the EDU Center.

John Crozier

John originally came to us as an intern from Southeast Christian Church. When we connected with Southeast in 1994, their philosophy was not to send American students as missionaries because they were concerned the kids might be more of a problem than a blessing. We understood as we had experienced a few negative situations, but I still thought it could work. Southeast was resistant, but I finally convinced them to give it a try. John was the first, and it's fair to say it's worked out well.

Southeast sent John, right out of college, to work for us for a few months. He went back to America but a couple of months later returned to Poland for a longer period of time. That was the start of a long-term relationship, and John is still an essential part of our ministry today. This also helped set up a long-term relationship with Southeast, sending young people to serve with us.

When John first came, Zaba was his boss. John helped us with a tea house we had in Warsaw, working with Rafal to organize discussions about films we showed.

Working under Zaba was the beginning of their relationship, and all these years later, they are still happily married.

Daniel And Edyta Wawrzyniak
Daniel is my nephew, and both he and his wife, Edyta, have been part of our ministry from the beginning.

Edyta was one of our early campers. She was not really interested and didn't listen to what the pastors were saying from the pulpit. But finally, one dynamic and very loud preacher got her attention; she finally listened, and she gave her life to Jesus.

Edyta and Daniel knew each other from high school, and their relationship grew as they experienced camp together each summer until they were finally married.

Edyta, by profession, is a physical therapist but joined our team doing office work and finances.

When Daniel graduated from school, he became involved in the amateur basketball league in Warsaw and started running our sports camps. Fifteen years later, Daniel has run just about every big event that's happened at Zakościele.

Rafal And Agnieszka Piekarski
Rafal and Agnieszka have also been with us from the beginning. Rafal connected with our ministry when he was invited to one of our music camps. Soon, he and Agnieszka moved to Warsaw for

college and served with us as camp counselors in the summer. A couple of years later, I had the privilege of marrying them.

Both studied linguistics and were preparing for jobs as professional translators, but after they got married, they decided to go do internships at Southeast Christian Church as part of our exchange program. They were there for a year, then returned and got involved in our camps. Rafal was helpful in all kinds of ways and showed amazing leadership potential.

Brian Wright, who I mentioned earlier, told me he was moving to Kansas City, where he would be helping launch a second campus of an existing church. I thought it might be time to send someone to learn about the process of planting a church. Rafal, Agnieszka, and their first child, Wojtek, went to Kansas City to get that experience.

When they returned, we sat under an apple tree. (I've found that the greatest conversations happen under apple trees.) Rafal shared his heart and desire, "I believe God is redirecting me to serve in a church." I didn't tell him, but I felt like we were losing them from Proem, and it was painful. Now, looking back at what God has done, it's obvious we didn't lose them at all. We added an essential new branch of our ministry.

We had just started meeting together on Sunday mornings in Tomaszów Mazowiecki, and Rafal stepped into the role of leading that church. He's still doing that today.

Agnieszka was a German teacher at the school. But after a few years, she felt called to change her profession to counseling and is now one of the two primary leaders for our Helps Ministry, along with Adam Pańczak.

Przemek And Agata Dwulat

Przemek and Agata, our son and daughter-in-law, are in leadership positions as well. Przemek heads up our IT media production, and Agata is involved in Exodus 15 and our worship music.

Obviously, Przemek grew up in our ministry. Like many of our staff, they were helping us even as kids and had leadership responsibilities before they became staff members. Przemek and Agata do our graphic and print materials. Agata, along with Alicja and Zaba, is a school director responsible for public relations.

Michał And Karolina Kupczyk

Michał and Karolina serve in the leadership of Exodus 15. They sing, write songs, and help with music at our school and church. They also grew up with us through our camps. We actually first met them at a basketball camp.

Tomek And Stephanie Gużda

Tomek is involved in filmmaking on our ministry's technology side. His wife, Stephanie, came to us as an intern from Southeast and now teaches at the school and serves as a counselor to the students.

I realize I'm in trouble because I have to stop at some point, but I could keep listing incredible, essential leaders in our ministry.

Today, we have approximately 150 staff members. They didn't all grow up in Proem, but they all share our values, which makes it possible to live out our third core value: team leadership.

Team Leadership

Our three distinctives are relationships first, process over product, and team leadership.

In the beginning, we didn't really practice team leadership because we didn't yet have a team. It was just me. But as soon as we could, and very intentionally, we moved from "Maui making the decisions" to "Maui plus." It's no longer just about me; what a blessing that is. It makes our organization so much healthier and stronger.

Some people outside of our ministry assume I'm still the primary decision-maker, but the truth is that we have a team of people who submitted to God and under the direction of the Holy Spirit, work together to lead Proem.

It's not just Maui.

In church planting, it's Maui plus Rafal.

For the school, it's Zaba and John and Alicja.

Agnieszka and Adam are the point leaders for the Helps Ministry.

Everything we do is team leadership.

Everyone has a different and needed perspective.

We make decisions within our relationships, and the process we use is very important. When we sit down together, we each bring our experiences to the table. We share our thoughts and then choose the best option together. We never vote. We trust God to lead us to 100 percent agreement, and as he does, we move forward. If someone isn't sure about a decision, we leave it for our next meeting.

For instance, there was a time when we were debating whether to open another camp in Poland or invest in a school. At that time, we knew how to do camps but not a school. It felt like choosing between an easy and a hard way, but we weren't sure. We continued to pray and share our opinions, and eventually, we all came to the conclusion that we needed to do a school.

We recently added a sports academy to our school, which has grown our sports ministry in a big way. We are about to open a music academy to help us reach out into the community. This year, we offered a trip to the Holy Land for the first time, as Rafal took forty people to see where Jesus lived and did ministry.

All of those were team decisions. I don't know if I would have come up with any of those ideas on my own, but I don't have to because we practice team leadership.

Maui's Leadership

This brings me, as we near the end of the book, to the topic of the end of my ministry.

I have been asked many times how long I plan to be involved in leadership with Proem, and the frequency is increasing as I get older.

I have no plans to step away. Being involved with these young people is keeping me young. I hope to continue serving at Proem for at least a few more years as long as I can make an impact. I look forward to every day I'm able to serve in the role God has given me.

But eventually there will come a day when I am no longer involved. When that day comes, I'll be proud of what God has accomplished through us in decades of ministry, and I will have no doubt our ministry will continue to thrive.

I love to be around, and I guess it might hurt my feelings if our leadership team said, "Maui, go retire in Florida because we're tired of you." But at the same time, they grew up in the ministry, currently lead the ministry, and could do so without me with no problem. My influence is diminishing, but our core leaders are multiplying what I have invested into their lives.

I've been asked which of our leaders would replace me. I don't think we'll have one person step into that role. Because of our commitment to team leadership, we have learned to work together in complementary roles. We each have our roles—areas of ministry in which we may be the point leader, and we all help each other succeed.

I think the most likely scenario when I'm gone is that each of our leaders will continue to run their own part of the ministry separately but keep doing all the ministry together. It's in our DNA to work together because it's like we've become wired together. Of course, each of us is different, and that's a good thing in a leadership team. There is no one like Rafal as a speaker. There is no one like John as a speaker. There is no one like Daniel, which is a good thing. (I'm joking, but there is definitely no one like Daniel.) There is no one like Przemek when it comes to attention to detail. I could go on and on.

Someone asked me recently, "Who will be like Maui, the visionary?" I appreciate the question, but I don't think we need another Maui. The vision has been cast, and our ministry is functioning well because we gauge everything by how it fits that vision.

I know I've played an essential role in our history, but my role is no longer indispensable. That's why I like to be called the founder rather than the director of the ministry. It's more accurate. In fact, when I go on a trip to another country, not only does our ministry not suffer, but it continues in exactly the same way without me.

When our ministry was about fifteen years old, a friend of mine asked me how long I thought I would keep working for Proem. I pondered that question for a moment and finally said, "When I turn sixty-two, I will retire, and someone else will lead."

When I turned sixty-two, I realized I was enjoying life more. I had developed my own leadership style and, more importantly, a leadership team. I knew I needed them more than they needed me. It's such a good feeling.

I feel good.

I feel safe.

I am now sixty-eight—a young sixty-eight. Officially, I'm at retirement age, but I still can't imagine stepping away. To do what? I'm not the typical person who reaches the age of retirement and is finally able to enjoy life. I enjoy life all the time. And I am enjoying my work more than ever, partly because I don't have so much to do because of our amazing next generation of leaders.

We have served together and each of us treasures our relationships with each other and with the people we serve.

What could possibly be better?

CONCLUSION

W e've reached the end of the book, but it's hardly the end of the story. God has so much more in store for Proem.

What will it be? What does the future hold?

I don't know.

It's interesting; looking back, I feel like nothing has changed, and everything has changed.

Nothing had changed in that back before Proem even really started; people would ask me for our vision. I would smile and say with all the confidence I could muster, "Proem exists to evangelize the lost, equip believers, and affect communities."

The same is true today. Nothing has changed.

On the other hand, *so much* has changed.

Evangelizing the lost used to happen almost entirely in the context of camps. Today, we share the Gospel in all kinds of ways, including having the biggest education center in Poland, whose real purpose is to share Christ.

Equipping believers used to happen primarily through a program after camps called "correspondence Bible course." We gave campers who made a decision for Jesus ten lessons to do at home and send back to us. Today, we equip in so many ways—including teaching and educational materials happening in three church locations, video lessons recorded by our media department, and weekly classes on how to communicate the Gospel. Adam Szumorek, PhD, who is the teaching pastor at TOMY church, has written eleven books to help believers grow in their faith.

Affecting communities started with gatherings in backyards and city parks but has grown into Kontakt, serve-the-city projects, and mission trips to other countries.

Looking back on our three-plus decades of ministry, Proem today is so much more than what we expected in 1990. What we were doing then is about 5 percent of what we're doing now, but the way we do it is 100 percent the same.

That leads to an exciting thought. If what we were doing in 1990 is 5 percent of what we're doing now, that means Proem is twenty times more impactful today than it was back then. Thirty years from now, Proem could be twenty times more impactful than what we're experiencing as I write this book in 2024.

So, what does the future hold? I don't know, but I trust God will do even more. I believe nothing will change, and so much will change.

It's all up to God. Our future is in his hands, and we trust him with it.

Thank you for caring enough about Proem to read this book. I pray God richly blesses you—with him, with his presence, his will, and a deep desire to be a part of bringing his kingdom to earth.

Speaking of which, I feel it would be appropriate to end this book with a prayer to the God who is responsible for everything that's happened in my life and through Proem.

Father God,

Thank you for each person who cares enough about Proem to have read this book. I pray you richly bless them with you—your presence, your will, a desire to be a part of bringing your kingdom to earth.

God, I thank you for all you've done in and through my life. You've been so gracious, shown me the way to go, and entrusted me with so much. You've surrounded me with an awesome family, leadership team, and ministry partners. I am so grateful.

I pray for the future of Proem that you will continue to do what you've been doing. But not just for me, Lord, for future generations. Jesus, you promised that your disciples would do even greater things than you, and my prayer is that they will do and experience greater things than I have.

God, I am fulfilled. I am satisfied. But I'm also ready for more. Not just for me, Lord, but for the next generation. I pray that you do even greater things after I'm gone, all to your glory.

But Lord, I pray you're not finished with me yet. I want your will done in my life, and I pray your will is that I will be able to serve you all my days, and that one night I'll fall asleep, still making an impact with Proem, and wake up in heaven.

I pray in Jesus's name.

Amen.

ABOUT THE AUTHOR

Wladyslaw "Maui" Dwulat was born in a time marked with uncertainty and the opportunity of fading Communism. With the precious gift of evangelical faith as his guide, he moved forward into an uncharted cultural and political landscape of emerging faith and possibility in a newly democratic Poland. A frontiersman at heart, his passion and undying belief that "the best is yet to come" coupled with "partnership in the spirit of togetherness" forged a path into the future for thousands of young Polish students who would gather to hear the Gospel for the first time at conferences and evangelical outreach camps in the 90's.

His focus on the next generation of young Polish youth and service as the General Secretary for the newly formed Evangelical Alliance in Poland helped to mobilize a new era of evangelical belief and values. As President of Festival of Hope for Poland and in cooperation with Franklin Graham and the Billy Graham Association, he helped usher in a new era of openness—filled with forgiveness, truth, and hope. His leadership and support of local

Christian Churches throughout Poland helped cement and bring together a movement focused on evangelism through practical community-based service, which continues today.

His life and his story (which you now hold in your hands) continue to inspire, invite, encourage, and challenge with a childlike faith and belief in a God who still today insists on doing the impossible, one life at a time—a life best understood and seen most clearly through the lives and ongoing ministry of so many who have benefitted from his personal words of encouragement and lived example over the last half-century.

ACKNOWLEDGMENTS

This book could not have been written, and the story may not have existed without the help of many people . . .

- So many people here in Poland, for whom the idea of doing a parachurch ministry was new due to the changes from communism to democracy, but who have prayed for us and supported us for decades.

- Names like Andrzej, Stefania, Krzysztof, Ewa, Henryk, Ryszard, Piotr, Władek, Urszula, Kazik, Halina, Dorota, Gienek, Józek . . . and many others who have are such a big part of the history of Proem.

- Brian Wright, who long ago heard me say, "Why not do it?!" This became his favorite refrain for Proem. He repeats it often, year after year. And so . . . we do it.

- A rare friend, Hal Heiner, whose primary question is always, "How can we help Proem?" and then steps up and helps.

- David Smale, who spent many hours with me and helped initiate this writing process.

- Vince Antonucci, master of the written word; there would be no book without him.

- Annette Peters for helping create the stateside entity of Proem Support Ministries, Inc., and for faithfully administering thousands of transactions and countless other critical organizational responsibilities.

- Karen Franczek, for her unconditional love, hospitality, and help—often with little notice.

- Stan Franczek, my dear friend and sounding board who has supported Proem for the past thirty years. Our relationship with Stan and Karen gives my wife Ewa and me life and lessons on how to love. I thank Stan for selflessly, spiritually, and financially assisting us with Proem's journey. God has done so much through our mutual efforts and involvement.

- This year, we are celebrating thirty years of partnership with Southeast Christian Church. I am so grateful for our spirit of togetherness and transparency as we carry out the work of the Lord with one another.

- My dear wife Ewa, without you, there is no me and no Proem. Your understanding and empathy change me and the world around us.

- Last, there are far too many to mention by name, but to all those who have prayed faithfully over the years for God's strength and blessing on Proem, thank you!

Made in the USA
Columbia, SC
13 November 2024

46466885R00102